Billy Humphrey has writt[en] [...] Church. *Unceasing* takes y[...] [...] through the Scriptures to offer a clear biblical basis for night-and-day prayer, as well as prophetic insight into God's end-time agenda for the prayer movement that is sweeping the globe. I recommend it to anyone whose heart is being stirred to pursue the Lord in prayer and fasting in this hour.

—Mike Bickle
Director, International House of Prayer, Kansas City, MO

The rumblings are everywhere. A surge of corporate prayer is exploding globally. Believers worldwide are asking questions like, "What's happening? Is it scriptural? Where is it going? Why should I get involved?" This is possibly the first book written specifically to answer these questions, and Billy Humphrey has the credentials to address them. A weighty book, released at a critical hour.

—Bob Sorge
Author, *Secrets of the Secret Place*

I am convinced that we live in the greatest hour of history. The glory of the Lord is rising on the Church and her light is shining brightly in the midst of darkness. God's heart longs for nations, and He is intent on giving His Son the inheritance He asked for. Because of this, God is on the move and stirring His people to give themselves fully to what He is doing in the earth. At the forefront of what God is doing is a global prayer movement rumbling through the nations. Night-and-day prayer is arising to God from every corner of the earth. Billy Humphrey is a modern-day revivalist who has given himself to a life of prayer and answered the high call of God to stand with Jesus in intercession. Billy's mandate to call people to a life of night-and-day prayer is not coming out of a theory, but has been birthed in the prayer room. In *Unceasing*, Billy expresses his mandate by calling us to engage in the global prayer movement. Billy's contribution to the worldwide prayer movement is unmistakable, and his passion for the heart of God is unquestionable.

—Banning Liebscher
Director, Jesus Culture, Sacramento, CA

Billy Humphrey has been branded by heaven with a vision for day-and-night prayer, and he makes a compelling case through Scripture and history that this is God's plan. My heart was stirred to live more deeply in the secret place as I absorbed the fresh, faith-building challenge of this book.

—Dr. Michael L. Brown
President, FIRE School of Ministry, Concord, NC

UNCEASING

AN INTRODUCTION TO NIGHT & DAY PRAYER

Billy Humphrey

With an introduction by Allen Hood

FORERUNNER
PUBLISHING
KANSAS CITY, MISSOURI

Unceasing: An Introduction to Night & Day Prayer
By Billy Humphrey

Published by Forerunner Publishing
International House of Prayer
3535 E. Red Bridge Road, Kansas City, MO 64137
ihopkc.org/books

Forerunner Publishing is the book-publishing division of the International House of Prayer of Kansas City, an evangelical missions organization that is committed to praying for the release of the fullness of God's
power and purpose, as we actively win the lost, heal the sick, feed the
poor, make disciples, and impact society.

ISBN: 978-0-9823262-3-7
eBook ISBN: 978-1-938060-23-6

Unless otherwise noted, scripture is taken from the *New King James Version*. Copyright © 1982 by Thomas Nelson Inc. Used by permission. All
rights reserved.

Scripture quotations marked (NIV) are taken from the *Holy Bible, New
International Version*, NIV*. Copyright © 1973, 1978, 1984, 2011 by
Biblica, Inc™. Used by permission of Zondervan. All rights reserved.

Scripture quotations marked (NASB) are taken from the *New American
Standard Bible*, copyright © 1960, 1962, 1963, 1968, 1971, 1972, 1973,
1975, 1977, 1995 by the Lockman Foundation. Used by permission.

Italics in quotations indicate emphasis by the author.
Cover art by Isaac Weisman
Interior design by Ian Barker
Printed in the United States of America

To my children, Evan, Siah, Coby, and Riah: You are forerunners living at the end of the age! I pray this book will give you understanding of the global end-time prayer movement. You are the love of my life.

Contents

Acknowledgments

I want to thank Mike Bickle and Lou Engle for blazing a trail in prayer that is challenging an entire generation to wholeheartedly pursue the Lord. I greatly appreciate their friendship and encouragement.

I am grateful to Bob Sorge for exhorting me to develop as a writer—for motivating me to stretch myself and continue to grow.

I want to thank Jono Hall for his input on the chapter "Historical Accounts of Night-and-Day Prayer." His research and writing have helped shape what I have written.

I want to thank Jamie Burns, Jules Tompkins, Lisa Garcia, and Wesley Huth for their efforts in helping me write this book. Their input, suggestions, and research on this project have greatly improved this work. Without their help, this book would not have become a reality.

I want to thank Jennifer Sansom and Maggie Syrett for their masterful editing. Their skill and insight were invaluable in sculpting the final manuscript.

Foreword

By Lou Engle

IN 1993, I READ AN article on prayer that prophesied that the Lord was going to raise up twenty-four-hour houses of prayer throughout the earth. The Lord gripped my heart with this vision. Three years later, He clearly told me to pray for the "Moravian lampstand" to be recommissioned. For 120 years, the fire of night-and-day prayer burned in Herrnhut, Germany, through a band of Moravian believers

The Lord later spoke clearly to us at TheCall, a prayer ministry I helped found. He said in a dream, "Wherever TheCall goes, I will establish My house of prayer." It is not enough to simply have breakthrough prayer meetings; we must sustain what we gain spiritually with continuous intercession and worship.

Now, over two decades later, I burn with anticipation as we are witnessing God beginning to fulfill His prophetic promises. He is rekindling the flame of prayer that the Moravians carried for over a century. All over the world, God is establishing houses of prayer built on unceasing intercession and worship.

I am convinced that 24/7 prayer is the necessary precursor to the greatest awakening the earth will ever see. A global fasting and prayer movement is rapidly gaining momentum—entire nations are being mobilized to cry out in intercession. What could be the outcome but an incredible harvest of souls and the return of the Lord Jesus Himself?

Unceasing is an invaluable resource to the Church. In this book, Billy Humphrey calls believers to follow in the footsteps of the prolific intercessors from the Bible as well as from church history.

I highly recommend *Unceasing* to anyone who is interested in the global prayer movement. You will be challenged to rethink your understanding of prayer and provoked to respond to the call of Joel 2 with fasting, weeping, and mourning.

I pray that you will be part of this restoration and that your heart will be set ablaze with God's vision for night-and-day prayer in this generation, so that we might truly see the prayer of Jesus answered: "Your kingdom come. Your will be done, on earth as it is in heaven" (Mt. 6:10).

Lou Engle
TheCall, Inc.

A Vision of Night-and-Day Prayer

By Allen Hood

"For from the rising of the sun, even to its going down, My name shall be great among the Gentiles; in every place incense shall be offered to My name, and a pure offering; for My name shall be great among the nations," says the LORD of hosts.

MALACHI 1:11

GOD IS LOOKING FOR UNCEASING adoration and perpetual prayer. To many of us, the prayer movement seems to have sprung from nowhere. At first it was just a few odd people on a hillside shouting that God was doing something new in raising up day-and-night prayer. At first, it was only "those people" calling for it. Yet what we have seen in the last generation is nothing short of electrifying. Unceasing adoration and perpetual prayer have exploded all over the world. No longer is it only a few groups here and there with an outlandish vision. Throughout the nations, people have been gripped with the vision for 24/7 prayer, and they are doing it.

I am continually amazed at what God is doing with prayer. It sparked out of nowhere and spread like a brushfire. Thousands of networks, houses of prayer, and praying churches are emerging all over the earth, so fast that we are hard-pressed to document what is happening. I was in Myanmar after Cyclone Nargis in 2008, and an Assemblies of God pastor rushed up to me and excitedly said, "IHOP! We saw you praying on the microphone over the webstream." With great joy he announced, "We're doing it!"

"What exactly are you doing?" I asked him.

"We are doing *it!*" he replied. "We bought twenty acres in the outskirts of Yangon. We have no electricity, so we purchased landscaping lights, put them in the ground, and on the weekend we worship Him all through the night. We are not going to stop until the nation is filled with the songs of the Lamb."

The passion and determination of this man astonished me. They had no building, no electricity, none of the comforts that in the developed world we take for granted, and yet there they are, driven by a passion to offer Jesus unceasing adoration, and devoting their lives to making it happen. But it doesn't stop there.

After Myanmar I flew to Hong Kong and found a similar story—believers in southern China and Hong Kong are committing themselves to the call of night-and-day prayer. I flew to Tauranga, New Zealand, and discovered that a church, a house of prayer, and a Youth with a Mission base had joined together, saying, "We don't know how this works, but we are going to raise up day-and-night prayer and worship in this part of the world." I was in Brazil during the week of Carnival and found 1,000 twenty-year-olds passionate to gather and give themselves to pray throughout the entire week. They were seeking God because they wanted to start 24/7 prayer in their nation while the world outside was celebrating in drunken debauchery.

Just thirty years ago there were a few lonely voices who carried the message of prayer to the church. The likes of E. M. Bounds (1835–1913) and Andrew Murray (1828–1917) were faithful in their generation; they died at the beginning of the last century and yet they remained the authorities on prayer. The rise of the prayer movement within the church has changed all that. These faithful messengers have remained influential, yet they have been joined by a new generation. Over the last thirty years we have watched as God has done something incredible in the earth. At first only a few prayer ministries sprang up here and there, but as time has gone on all manner of types and models of the prayer ministry have arisen. Now, as we look across the globe, we see houses of prayer, prayer towers, "Luke18" campus ministries, praying churches, ministries across cities gathering for sustained prayer, people meeting in houses and fields and dorm rooms, seeking God together.

Prayer is exploding, as we have grown from near prayerlessness to more informed and prophetic intercession concerning nations and people groups, with the 10/40 Window initiative for the Middle East and Asia and the 4/14 Window initiative for children between the ages of four and fourteen. The Holy Spirit is presently drawing our attention back to the Holy Land—to praying for the salvation of Israel and the Jewish people. We are watching in awe as we see God respond to our concerted prayer. The gospel is going forth all over the earth and entire cities are being transformed by Jesus Christ.

I believe what we have witnessed with the Global Day of Prayer over the past ten years has been something of a high point in the prayer movement. In 2001, Graham Power, director of the Global Day of Prayer, had a vision to bring churches in South Africa together from across denominational lines to repent before the Lord and seek God together.[1] The classic text from 2 Chronicles 7:14 was his motivation: "If My people who are called by My name will humble themselves, and pray and seek My face, and turn from their wicked ways, then I will hear from heaven, and will forgive their sin and heal their land."

It grew from South Africa and spread to the entire African continent; from there it reached hundreds of countries around the world, until in 2009 over 220 nations and provinces in the world were participating in the Global Day of Prayer in some form. Some said that as many as three hundred million believers gathered in stadiums around the world to pray in unity for the outpouring of the Holy Spirit upon all flesh[2] and for the fulfillment of the Great Commission.[3]

Wherever we see focused and concerted prayer arising, we find that the saints are not satisfied with weekly or even daily prayer meetings, they are discontent with daily prayer meetings. The people participating in these prayer ministries are growing hungrier for the Lord and the release of His glory, and they are pushing passionately for day-and-night, 24/7 prayer. They do not want it only in their churches and cities; they want to see 24/7 in every tribe, nation, and tongue, until Jesus Christ returns to reign over the nations of the earth.

As I have pondered all that I have seen happening and dialoged with the Lord over this shift, I feel this significant transition that is happening in the body of Christ was shown nowhere more clearly than at the World Prayer Assembly, which took place in 2012. Outside Jakarta, Indonesia, over one million people gathered in fifteen stadiums for three days to seek God and pray. This was hugely significant; in the middle of the largest Muslim nation in the world, these Christians were together, crying out to God, asking Him to break in and transform their nation with the gospel of Jesus Christ.

When Graham Power rose to the platform and addressed the people, his message and challenge concerned the rising tide of night-and-day prayer. He summarized the growth of prayer in the church over the last few decades, and then announced that the next move of prayer in the church would be night-and-day prayer in every tribe and tongue, until the Lord returned. If Power had made this announcement thirty years ago, most of the people would have remained unusually quiet, not understanding such a strange idea. But I was shocked by what happened next. The stadium roared its approval. Instead of responding with hesitancy and skepticism, believers are ready and excited. Praying people all over the world are chomping at the bit, researching, and asking God how they might begin 24/7 prayer in their cities. As I watched the crowd cheer at the idea of a global 24/7 prayer movement that day, I knew something had changed in the body of Jesus, and whereas before the Global Day of Prayer had seemed like the ceiling, a high point in our experience, it was now steadily becoming a floor, and the beginning of a prayer journey. The vision had been growing for many years, but now a man with spiritual authority was giving credence to it. He was charging the body of Christ with the vision, and she responded gloriously.

Is Night-and-Day Prayer Permissible?

As we begin to think about a global prayer movement, it is important that we lay a scriptural and ecclesiological foundation for the practice of night-and-day prayer. It is easy to get excited about the prospect of unceasing adoration; however, many leaders and careful laymen are wondering if it is even biblical. Many are ready to begin pushing for night-and-day prayer in their hometowns and churches, but they want to know whether this is truly God-ordained. Is there a biblical basis for corporate gatherings of night-and-day prayer? Is there a precedent in church history?

After careful study, I can respond with a resounding yes! Perhaps the best way to start is with the basic question of whether 24/7 prayer is permissible. This is a question I am asked frequently. Is the church *allowed* to do such a thing? Is this not moving beyond the bounds of New Testament ecclesiology? Many times, after a long discussion, the question is boiled down to an issue of safety. Is this kind of ministry potentially dangerous to the health and sustainability of the local church?

I think the simplest answer is that unceasing adoration and perpetual prayer are never prohibited in Scripture; in fact, extravagant worship is only encouraged and praised. An example of this is seen in the non-compulsory vow of the Nazirite, in Numbers 6:1–21, where provision is made for those men and women who desire to go beyond the bounds of the Mosaic covenant in their devotion to God. In the Old Testament, particularly in Genesis, we find people building altars of worship before the Lord. Most are built *voluntarily* by the worshiper;[4] they were not prescribed by God, and yet it seems that God rewards such displays of extravagant worship.

Probably the clearest example of a person going outside the bounds of prescribed worship is King David, with his desire to build a house for God. When, in 2 Samuel 7, David came to rest in his own house in Jerusalem after bringing the ark of the covenant up to Zion, he spoke with Nathan the prophet, telling him, "See now, I dwell in a house of cedar, but the ark of God dwells inside tent curtains."[5] David was uncomfortable with the fact that while he dwelt in a permanent home of cedar wood, the ark of God rested under a tent made of animal skins. David wasn't commanded, but he couldn't help the dream of his heart for a temple in Jerusalem where the ark could rest and where YHWH could be worshiped by His people. Nathan perceived David's desires and assured him that God would be with him if he built a temple for the ark.

Later, David was told that he was not the one to build a temple for the Lord—it would be built by one of his sons. Although the building of the physical temple was not entrusted to David, the establishment of the order of worship that took place in the temple was. And here we find another example of David's extravagant and unprecedented devotion.

The Davidic order of worship is first seen in the tabernacle that David established in Jerusalem, where day-and-night prayer was undertaken by thousands of singers and musicians.[6] (It should be noted that the tabernacle of David is perhaps the *first biblical precedent for day-and-night worship*). David brought the ark of the covenant into Jerusalem and set it up in a tent, where he, the priests, and the Levites had open access to God, day and night.[7] We have no evidence that God had required this of David yet, but it seems clear that this order of worship was already in the heart of God, and it soon beat in the heart of David. David's act of placing the resources of Israel in the service of YHWH through thousands of ministers in the tabernacle on Mount Zion is an action of extravagance that God loved. The wonderful thing about both the tabernacle and the temple is that neither of these examples of worship were initially commanded by God, and yet He loved and blessed both expressions of extravagant worship, and caused both to prosper.

After David passed on, we find the Davidic order of worship instituted and reinstituted during the various high points and revivals in Judah's history. Solomon reestablished the Davidic order with the opening of the Temple.[8] Jehoshaphat, Joash, Hezekiah, and Josiah all sought to restore the priests, singers, and musicians to 24/7 service inside the temple as part of their national repentance.[9] After more than seventy years of captivity in Babylon, Ezra and Nehemiah worked hard to restore the temple and the walls of the city. When the temple was ready for service, the Davidic order of perpetual prayer and worship was reinstated.[10]

In answering the question of whether 24/7 worship is permissible, we find that the witness of Scripture gives an affirmative answer. Yet it is also possible to look at the witness of church history. Through the centuries, the church has seen a push for day-and-night prayer; she has explored what the corporate implications of Paul's command to "pray without ceasing"[11] might look like. We can see this in the various monastic traditions throughout the Middle East, North Africa, and Europe.

We can see this in Egyptian monks, Syrian monks, and Irish monks, who devoted themselves to what became known in the Catholic tradition as *laus perennis*, or perpetual praise, and not for a few years, but for centuries. We can see it in eighteenth-century Germany with a group of Moravian refugees and a rich young ruler by the name of Zinzendorf, whose "hourly intercessions" led to a night-and-day prayer movement that fueled the first Protestant missions movement. It is a simple fact of history that each of these prayer furnaces inevitably led to evangelistic outreach. Each missionary thrust moved further than almost anyone was willing to go at the time. From the revivals in Israel after the reinstitution of the Davidic order to the Moravians who sold themselves into slavery to preach the gospel where it was unwelcome, the tie between perpetual prayer and world missions is undeniable.

We see the same fruit in our own day with the prayer mountains that have blossomed in South Korea in the past fifty years. Touching the heart of God in prayer always leads to a unified people who follow the Great Commission of Jesus. We see the good fruit of prayer born time and again through the centuries, and as this age draws to a close, we will see the largest missions movement the world has known. In that day we will see the people "sing to the Lord a new song, His praise from the end of the earth," all those "who go down to the sea, and all that fills it, the coastlands and their inhabitants."[12] The deserts and the cities, people from every tribe and nation, language and people will be praying and singing to the Lord.

On Earth as It Is in Heaven

Another question we must ask is, why now? Why is the Lord raising the prayer movement up so rapidly at this time in history?

Night-and-day prayer is an answer to the prayer Jesus gave His church: "Our Father in heaven, hallowed be Your name. *Your kingdom come. Your will be done on earth as it is in heaven.*"[13] Right now, if the veil thinned and we found ourselves on the sea of glass, we would see two things: unceasing adoration and perpetual prayer. We would witness the four living creatures circling the throne in endless flight, covering their faces and feet, gazing at the Beautiful One on His throne, and singing out, "Holy, Holy, Holy!" While the four living creatures sing their song, twenty-four elders would be falling down before the glory of God, proclaiming with loud voices, "You are worthy, O Lord, to receive glory and honor and power!" This they do, day and night, without rest.[14] At the center of it all we would see the slain Lamb, leading the eternal prayer and intercession service. The book of Hebrews has Jesus saying to His Father, "I will declare Your name to My brethren; in the midst of the assembly I will sing praise to You."[15] In saying "brethren,"

Jesus is referring to you and me. In Hebrews we learn that Jesus "always lives to make intercession."[16]

Indeed, God rules His heavenly government from the context of night-and-day prayer. Intercession is the method the Father has given to Jesus to become ruler over the nations; "*Ask of Me,* and I will give You the nations for Your inheritance, and the ends of the earth for Your possession."[17] Right along with Jesus' intercession we see the attendants at the throne partnering with divine prayer: "Worthy is the Lamb who was slain to receive power and riches and wisdom, and strength and honor and glory and blessing!" This is at once a statement of praise to Jesus and intercession to God, that He would give these to Jesus.

If we are going to take seriously the kingdom mandate, we must take account for the manner in which He rules; we cannot bypass it. If we truly desire that His kingdom come and His will be done on earth as it is in heaven, we must understand that it will not look different to the scene in Revelation 4 and 5. Then we can align ourselves with it, and participate in the prayer and worship service of the throne room.

At this point many will be thinking, "But I can't do this. I don't have time to spend hours a day in a prayer room." We have seen in recent years the idea of "seven spheres" of society, meaning that there are seven main areas in society to be touched by the gospel of Jesus Christ: in no particular order, business, arts and entertainment, education, family, government, media, and religion. What does this mean for our discussion? Simply put, everyone in the church, no matter where you are or what your vocation, has a part to play. The prayer and worship movement has a place for everyone in the Body of Christ, whether you have one hour or six hours a day to give. No one person can pray for everything. You have unique insight into the world situation based on where you live and work and play. God has invited you to join in with His global movement and contribute your voice to the growing cry over the earth, "Come, Lord Jesus!" Remember, this is what Jesus is doing. He is interceding now at the Father's throne until all His enemies are made a footstool for His feet.[18] Why not join Him in His intercession?

Moses and David saw glimpses into the heavenly throne room and understood that God rules as King through prayer and worship. Each of these beloved rulers of Israel established a priestly ministry before the Lord, in which the fire on the altar would not go out.[19] Both these leaders took Israel to heights not reached under any other leader. It must be noted that long before the kingship of Israel was established, the priesthood was put in place. In order of priority, it seems God is more concerned with priestly service than political rule, though I assure you, Jesus will reign as King-Priest over the world.[20]

We even see the first Christians participating in this. The New Testament church was born in the context of perpetual adoration. The apostles gathered the faithful into Solomon's Porch daily in the temple, the place Jesus called the "house of prayer for all nations."[21] We often remember the early believers met house to house, eating together, and too quickly forget they were also "continuing daily with one accord *in the temple*."[22] What was going on in the temple? Prayer and worship! And it was in this context that "the Lord added to the church daily those who were being saved."[23] The temple services were such a normal part of the Jerusalem church's life that Paul even paid four men's Nazirite fees in the temple.[24]

This is all worthy of our attention and careful consideration. New Testament ecclesiology certainly has room for perpetual worship, John saw it in the heavenly throne room, and we know that God wants to bring it from heaven to the earth.

It's Permissible, but Is It Necessary?

The last answer I have to questions about the legitimacy of the prayer movement is itself a question. So I ask, "Is not God worthy of worship and glory at every hour, day and night?" The power of this question lies behind its simplicity and the obvious answer. If for no other reason, the only fitting response to the infinite glory of the Triune God, the infinite worth of Jesus, is unceasing adoration.

I have had sincere pastors, concerned for their flocks, ask me, "Is 24/7 really necessary?" My answer is "No, it is not necessary—it is our privilege!" We do not *have* to do it, but we are invited into it. Day and night is our constraint and our limitation. God is worth twenty-*five* hours a day, three hundred and sixty-*seven* days a year if we could give it to Him. Imagine walking into the throne room of the living God, tapping one of the four living creatures on the shoulder, and saying, "Excuse me, sir. Is this really necessary?" Ask any living creature or anyone positioned before God on the sea of glass, and they will let you know that "necessity" is the wrong word. This is our inheritance. This is our privilege and glory.

We must also ask ourselves why, when God shows a glimpse into heaven, does He choose to show us the worship and prayer ministry? Why, when we are so eager for new strategies and new authority, does God not even show us the administration of that ministry? The only methodology we are given is night-and-day prayer and worship. Divine priority is yet again opposed to the wisdom of men. We must wrestle with this as pastors and laymen, theologians and blue-collar workers. The implications are massive. Again, imagine tapping a living creature on the shoulder, asking if this is necessary, or imbalanced. He would waste only one of his thousands of eyes, turn to you and ask, "Are we looking at the same God?" He would take you and point your two eyes at the eternal glory of God and say, "Just gaze at Him." You would be undone and would worship with him there for all eternity.

Returning to the scripture in Malachi, it is crucial to understand that it was written to the priests. Over and over again, God is accusing them of profaning His glory by their lack of zeal in the temple service. And He repeatedly attributes their neglect to their lack of concern for His greatness. We have much to learn from Malachi's prophecy. As you wrestle with these things I encourage you to read Malachi and to hear God calling you to take your place as priest before Him.[25] Let Malachi's rebukes work their way into your heart. Often we shy away from extravagant devotion because we are blind to the glory of God. We cover our blindness with cries for balance and safety and good theology, when we should be crying with the blind man, "Jesus, Son of David, have mercy on me!"[26]

O, Holy Spirit, open our eyes to see the beauty, glory, and majesty of this great God, Yahweh, and His Son, Jesus Christ!

All Israel Shall Be Saved

We must look at one more issue; we must look at the issue of Israel. In Romans 11:26 Paul utters an amazing promise, "And so all Israel will be saved." This is amazing, because in the preceding verses he was speaking about their blindness to the gospel. The question before us is this: if they are blind, how will all Israel be saved?

Isaiah 62 connects the global prayer movement to the salvation of Israel. God declares there that for Jerusalem's sake He will neither hold His peace nor rest until "her righteousness goes forth as brightness, and her salvation as a lamp that burns."[27] This is saying that God is committed to her salvation and glorification, that He is doing whatever it takes to bring her from the depths of shame, depression, and depravity to the heights of His own glory. He is not resting; He is working towards this, day and night. A few verses later God tells Jerusalem that He is not working alone: "I have set watchmen on your walls, O Jerusalem; *they shall never hold their peace day or night.*" He continues, instructing the watchmen, "You who make mention of the Lord, *do not keep silent, and give Him no rest* till He establishes and till He makes Jerusalem a praise in the earth."[28] This is about people from every language, tribe, people, and nation coming to the Lord, culminating with the entire nation of Israel bowing before their Messiah, Yeshua, and receiving His salvation. Years ago, when God first called my family to the prayer ministry in Kansas City, He made it clear, though He would move powerfully in the Midwest, that the climax of this movement would be unceasing intercession for Israel until they all received their Messiah.

This is why 24/7 is a necessity in the earth. We need it to see the greatest breakthrough of God's glory in Christian history, so that all Israel might be saved. Jesus makes this poignant point in His parable of the widow and the unjust judge, found in Luke 18. "He spoke a parable to them, *that men always ought to pray and not lose heart.*"[29] Through the parable Jesus says that God will act swiftly on behalf of those who cry out to Him "day and night."[30] Again, day-and-night prayer is shown to be the way God works. Jesus then asks a haunting question, "Nevertheless, when the Son of Man comes, will He really find faith on the earth?"[31]

I don't know that Jesus is asking so much *if* He will find this faith as *who* will have this faith that cries out to Him day and night for the release of justice. I tell you, Jesus will find this faith on the earth. Will He find it in me? Will He find it in you?

The global village is ready for 24/7. You can look up 24/7 on the Internet and find business, banking, industry, and services available at any hour. Department stores and food chains are opening 24/7. The world is restless, looking for something that satisfies at all hours of the day. Is it an accident that the fulfillment of the Great Commission is before us in a world that expects to be going all day and all night? Our cities and nations should have a place of refuge at 3:00am. I believe the prayer movement is one of the greatest efforts of God to detox a generation from the spirit of the age. And from it will emerge a missionary force never before imagined. We are ready for day-and-night worship and prayer. The world is hungry for it. God desires it.

Father, on earth as it is in heaven!

Notes

1. http://www.globaldayofprayer.com/index.php/about-us/history/.

2. See Joel 2:12–32 and Acts 2:17–21.

3. See Matthew 24:14.

4. See Genesis 8:20; 12:7–8; 13:18; 26:25; 33:20; and 35:3 for a few examples.

5. 2 Samuel 7:2.

6. 1 Chronicles 23:5; see also 1 Chronicles 9:33; 15:16–19; 16:4–7, 42.

7. 2 Samuel 6, 7.

8. 2 Chronicles 8:14–15.

9. See 2 Chronicles 20:20–22, 28; 23:1–24:27; 29:1–36; 30:21; 35:1–27.

10. Ezra 3:10; Nehemiah 12:28–47.

11. 1 Thessalonians 5:17.

12. See Isaiah 42:10–12.

13. Matthew 6:9–10.

14. See Revelation 4:6–11.

15. Hebrews 2:12.

16. Hebrews 7:25.

17. Psalm 2:8.

18. See Psalm 110.

19. See Leviticus 6:13.

20. See Psalm 110:4.

21. Matthew 21:13; Mark 11:17; Luke 19:46.

22. Acts 2:46.

23. Acts 2:47.

24. Acts 21:23–24.

25. 1 Peter 2:9.

26. Luke 18:38–39.

27. Isaiah 62:1.

28. Isaiah 62:6–7.

29. Luke 18:1.

30. Luke 18:7.

31. Luke 18:8.

$$\boxed{1}$$

It's Happening

"For from the rising of the sun even to its setting, My name will be great among the nations, and in every place incense is going to be offered to My name."

MALACHI 1:11, NASB

THE SIGN ABOVE THE DOOR was inscribed in traditional Chinese characters. "Do not enter unless you are serious about taking your watch." I asked my host, the local pastor, if I could go in; with a sign like that I didn't want to presume anything. He graciously nodded, opening the door.

I entered to find the room small and cold, the floor lined with children's multicolored cushion squares. In the center, two Chinese aunties were on their knees, weeping in prayer, their Bibles spread open before them. The presence of the Lord filled the place and arrested my senses. All I could think was, "This is holy!" The women soon asked me to pray for them. My response? "I need *you* to pray for *me*."

It was one of those moments I knew I would remember for the rest of my life. All that I'd preached and believed about the emerging global prayer movement was in evidence before my eyes. Here in this remote underground Chinese house church, night-and-day prayer was ascending before the Lord. Weeping, I fell to my knees as the weight of the moment bore upon me. How could it be? They had no knowledge of *any* of the modern Western ministries focused on night-and-day worship and prayer.

Until that moment, I had not understood the sovereign element of the expansion of the prayer movement. I knew it was growing rapidly, with many houses of prayer springing up across the globe. The International House of Prayer of Kansas City and 24-7 Prayer in Europe had inspired many to start similar ministries. But here, beyond the sound of any Western influence, these Chinese believers were burning for Jesus night and day.

I had spent the previous decade calling as many people as possible to engage in night-and-day prayer, all the while believing that God was initiating a global movement of prayer that would culminate in massive revival and the return of His Son. Seeing these Chinese house church believers practicing the very things I and many others had been preaching sent a shock of revelation through me: *It's all real! It's truly happening! God is doing it!* Even here He is setting watchmen on the wall night and day, until He comes and makes Jerusalem the praise of the earth.

The day before I encountered that tiny Chinese prayer room I had a secret meeting in a hotel three hours away. My contact, who was visibly shaken because of the security risk of publicly meeting with a Westerner, told me that her church ran a house of prayer that had been going 24/7 for the last sixteen months. I was sure my translator had misinterpreted what she said. Sometimes things are lost in translation, especially from English to Mandarin. I asked her several times, in different ways, to tell me about their prayer ministry. When she informed me of over twenty houses of prayer that were all 24/7 in their church (a network of approximately 7 million people), I was *sure* there was a misunderstanding. Finally, frustrated by my insistent questioning, she said, "Enough! Tomorrow you will see!"

Could it be? Were there really more than twenty 24/7 houses of prayer in this remote Chinese house church network?

After seeing it with my own eyes, I realized everything she had told me was real. That afternoon I had lunch with the local pastor. Trying to be as respectful as possible, but consumed with curiosity, I peppered him with questions about their houses of prayer: "How long have you been going? How many houses of prayer are in your network? Are they all 24/7? Have you ever heard of the International House of Prayer or Mike Bickle?"

His answers surprised me. They had twenty-four houses of prayer in their network that all had the commission to be twenty-four hours a day. As far as he knew, they were all operating around the clock. But they had no knowledge of any other 24/7 prayer ministries and had definitely never heard of any Western prayer or worship leaders. In fact, I was the first Westerner to preach in their local church in over a decade. The answer to my next question convinced me that their vision for night-and-day prayer had come from God and God alone.

"So how did you get the vision for night-and-day prayer?" I asked.

"Previous generations of our leaders have long had a vision to see the gospel touch all the nations and ultimately go back to Jerusalem. We always believed that if the gospel was to go all the way back to Jerusalem, it would require the power of night-and-day prayer to make it happen. Our leader told us to build night-and-day prayer throughout our church network, and so we did."

So simple, yet so profound—it was a vision God had birthed in the hearts of their leaders, and it now had become a reality.

The pastor's answer caused truths I had believed with my head to explode in my heart. Scriptures began to echo through my mind:

> "In every place incense shall be offered to My name . . . for My name shall be great among the nations." (Malachi 1:11)

> "I have set watchmen on your walls, O Jerusalem; they shall never hold their peace day or night." (Isaiah 62:6)

"This gospel of the kingdom will be preached in all the world
as a witness to all the nations, and then the end will come."
(Matthew 24:14)

The truth I thought I believed suddenly became even clearer—
God was raising up a *global* prayer movement that would touch
the ends of the earth to thrust forth the gospel throughout the
nations and set the stage for the coming of the Lord. It was really
happening!

Over a decade earlier, the Lord had begun to deal with me
about planting a house of prayer in Atlanta, Georgia. I had heard
of the International House of Prayer in Kansas City, but I knew
very little about the ministry. Through a series of events orches-
trated by the Lord, He made it clear to me that I was to move to
Kansas City, learn the message and model of the house of prayer,
and return to Atlanta to build a 24/7 worship and prayer ministry.

As I embarked upon this vision, God began to open the Scriptures to me in a way I had never experienced. His plan to establish
night-and-day prayer across the nations emerged from the pages
of my Bible. I began to understand that a massive movement of
prayer would be released in the earth alongside the global proclamation of the gospel, precipitating a great harvest of souls and
the return of the Lord.

Today, I lead a community of believers who have been engaging in ceaseless worship and prayer since 2006. In answer to our
prayers, God has begun to send forth laborers from our house of
prayer to multiple nations of the earth. What's more, this pattern of
prayer and proclamation is not confined to our local community,
but is being replicated in churches, missions organizations, and
ministries around the globe.

Night-and-day prayer is sweeping the nations. It's really happening. From little houses of prayer, to churches establishing a culture
of prayer, and missions bases housing hundreds of missionaries,
prayer initiatives are dotting the map.

Every great move of God's Spirit has been preceded by a great movement of prayer. I believe that the emergence of the global prayer movement is a sign of God's intention to release another great awakening. I'm convinced that God has reserved the greatest move of His Spirit for a day just ahead, and you and I are invited to partner with Him in it.

Perhaps you are like me, and the cry for "more" resounds from the depths of your being. Or maybe you have recently been stirred to seek God in prayer in a greater way than you have before. Or possibly the rising tide of night-and-day prayer in the earth has piqued your interest, drawing you to investigate what's written in the pages of this book.

Whatever the case, each of us has a unique journey that has brought us to this moment. We are at the onset of a global wave of prayer that will culminate in global revival and, ultimately, the return of the Lord. We are peering over a precipice at the greatest hour in human history.

In these pages we will go on a journey to investigate the prophetic, historical, and biblical foundations of the prayer movement that is sweeping the earth. It could be that you, like me, are called to pursue God in prayer until His presence once again possesses His people, until "good" prayer meetings give way to glory, until the gospel reaches every tribe, tongue, people and nation, and until He judges the earth, avenging His bride, taking the nations as His inheritance. This is truly a most incredible hour!

My visit to that underground house of prayer in China served to firmly cement the ideas that are held in these pages. God is really doing it, and He is inviting you and me to be a part of it. My prayer for you as you read this book is that God will make clear to you His agenda in this hour and your part in the emerging global prayer movement.

2

The Origins of the Tabernacle of David

So Samuel did what the LORD said, and went to Bethlehem. And the elders of the town trembled at his coming, and said, "Do you come peaceably?"

1 SAMUEL 16:4

WHEN GOD HIGHLIGHTS AN INDIVIDUAL in the Bible, we should take special notice. He is not so much drawing attention to the person, as using their life to demonstrate His own heart and ways, taking us through their life to teach us what is important to Him. David is one such character. Through God's dealings with David we gain great insight into what is important to God and how He works in the hearts of His people to bring His plans to pass.

Our journey into understanding the biblical precedents for night-and-day prayer starts with considering God's dealings with David. As we see the great focus and care God placed upon David's life and His commission to build night-and-day prayer, it will instruct us in God's ways and His desire for ceaseless worship from His people.

Imagine the day when Samuel, the Lord's prophet, approached the unremarkable village of Bethlehem. Bethlehem was one of the least important cities of Judah, and now one of the greatest prophets Israel had ever known was on his way.

Samuel was incredibly powerful. He had never given a prophecy that had not come to pass—"The Lord was with him and let none of his words fall to the ground" (1 Samuel 3:19). He was renowned throughout the nation. Once, as Samuel proclaimed the word of the Lord, God released supernatural thunder upon the Philistines that was so mighty it threw them into a state of confusion and fear, ultimately bringing about their defeat. Because of Samuel's powerful prophetic ministry, the Philistines were driven away from the towns of Israel throughout the entirety of his life.[1]

Undoubtedly his purpose in coming to tiny Bethlehem was to deliver a prophetic oracle that would have great impact upon the people. His very presence was fearsome. No wonder the town elders trembled at his coming!

Instead of making a great proclamation throughout the city, Samuel visited a simple townsman named Jesse. There is no record that Samuel had had any previous dealings with Jesse, who must have been astonished—this powerful prophet had come to his town, called him by name, and gathered the town elders together to attend a sacrifice in his home! What could it all mean?

Samuel told Jesse to summon his sons, so Jesse brought each one before the great prophet. But after seven sons had passed before his eyes, Samuel knew by the Spirit of the Lord that one was still missing.

"Are these all the sons you have?" Samuel asked.

"There is still the youngest, but he is tending the sheep," Jesse said with a hint of embarrassment.

"We will not sit down until he arrives," Samuel replied, convinced that this one would be the Lord's choice.

How could the young, red-haired shepherd boy who had been disregarded by his father comprehend what was about to happen? He was from the least significant town of his tribe, Judah, and he was the least within his family. Yet the days and nights he had spent faithfully serving his father's house, worshiping with his harp while watching over his father's sheep, had qualified him to be God's choice to shepherd His people Israel. Imagine David's shock at the gathering, when Samuel stepped forward and poured the horn of oil over him, anointing him in the name of the Lord as king of Israel.

Promotion and Demotion

> And David behaved wisely in all his ways, and the LORD was with him. (1 Samuel 18:14)

David's life was turned upside down from that moment forward. He was supernaturally empowered in all that he did. As a teen defending his father's sheep, he killed a lion and a bear with his bare hands. He was an anointed musician, who, with a song, could drive demons from those who were tormented.

As a young man, God anointed him to defeat Goliath, the mightiest warrior of the Philistines. As a result, when he was nearly twenty years old, King Saul appointed him as captain over the entire military force of Israel. The whole nation rallied around him. Even the young women wrote songs about his great exploits. What an amazing turn of events! God took David from watching sheep in the forgotten town of Bethlehem to commanding all the forces of Israel, even leading the nation in powerful military victories.

This was not the only dramatic turnaround that young David would experience. As quickly as he grew in popularity with the people, he became an object of scorn and hatred to Saul. The anointing and favor of God upon David's life infuriated Saul. As Saul recognized God's favor upon David, he feared that David would replace him as king. David's greatest ally morphed into his greatest enemy almost overnight. Seething with jealousy, Saul demoted David, removed him from his court, and attempted to murder him. As a result, David fled for his life, and Saul issued a command to all of his servants that if one of them should find David, they were to kill him.

David Flees to Ramah

> So David fled and escaped, and went to Samuel at Ramah, and
> told him all that Saul had done to him. And he and Samuel
> went and stayed in Naioth. (1 Samuel 19:18)

Rather than being the valiant commander of Israel's army, David
was now a fugitive whom the army commanders were seeking to
assassinate. David had experienced a roller-coaster ride of success
and rejection. He was completely alienated from the men he once
led. And worse, the man he had considered to be a spiritual father
now sought his life. In the face of these troubling and painful
circumstances, David turned to the man who was responsible for
initiating these events—Samuel.

For many years Samuel had lived in his hometown of Ramah,
where he had developed a school of the prophets, discipling young
men with prophetic giftings in worship, prayer, and prophecy. When
David arrived in Ramah, he told Samuel all that had transpired
between him and Saul.

Within a short time, Saul heard that David was in Ramah and
sent assassins to murder him, but the Spirit of the Lord divinely
intercepted them. As they approached, the power of God came
upon them and they began to prophesy the word of the Lord.
Upon returning to Saul, they explained to him why they had not
completed their assignment.

Saul sent two more groups of assassins to execute David. Each
time, the Spirit of the Lord intercepted them, causing them to
prophesy. It is likely that Saul was curious about these prophecies
and inquired of his men what it was that God caused them to
proclaim. Perhaps they prophesied the very thing that Samuel had
prophesied over David years earlier in Bethlehem: "David will be
king and ascend to the throne of Israel." Imagine how that must
have infuriated Saul!

Determined to destroy David, Saul took matters into his own hands. He traveled to Ramah himself, but just as with his assassins, the Spirit of the Lord came upon him and he prophesied all night under the influence of the Spirit of God. Perhaps he too prophesied David's kingship!

Unprecedented spiritual activity was taking place in Ramah. What was so important to God that He would pour out His Spirit upon executioners and transform them into oracles? What was the Lord doing through this powerful manifestation of His Spirit?

David's time spent with the prophet Samuel must have been extremely important. Ramah was approximately twenty miles from Gibeah, where Saul was stationed. It would have taken a few weeks for Saul to learn of David's presence in Ramah, send three envoys of assassins, and finally travel there himself. So at a minimum, David must have stayed there for several weeks.

What did David and Samuel talk about while he was there? It was something so essential, so monumental to the kingdom of God, that the Lord saw to it that no man's wicked plan could thwart His purposes. First Chronicles 9:22 conveys a hint of this vitally important meeting.

Blueprints for the Tabernacle

All those chosen as gatekeepers were two hundred and twelve. They were recorded by their genealogy, in their villages. David and Samuel the seer had appointed them to their trusted office. (1 Chronicles 9:22)

The tabernacle of David was a tent that housed a night-and-day worship and prayer meeting before the ark of the Lord. We are told that it was Samuel and David who initially formulated the plans and strategy for this first house of prayer. Together they looked through the genealogy of Israel to determine who should serve in the tabernacle of David. But Samuel died many years before the tabernacle was actually built.[2] When, then, did Samuel and David conceive of the plan for the tabernacle? It must have been while David was in Ramah. Other than David's anointing in Bethlehem, there is no other biblical account of David and Samuel spending *any* time together, so it is likely that the plans for the tabernacle of David were drawn up while David was in Ramah. When God thwarted Saul and his assassins, He was protecting the planning meeting for night-and-day prayer, which was to be established as the centerpiece of the kingdom of Israel.

Though David had fled to Ramah, hoping Samuel would get him out of trouble with Saul, God had quite a different plan. Perhaps David's dialogue with Samuel went something like this:

"Samuel, what did you do to me? After you anointed me, everything in my life changed. For a little while, things were great. I was stronger than ever. I killed a lion, a bear, and great warriors with ease. I was promoted in the military and became head of the armed forces. On top of that, my singing and playing improved; I was anointed for worship like never before. Demons began to flee when I played my harp. It was incredible—until Saul decided I was his enemy. What do I do now? I am a fugitive, and Saul's assassins are after me. They've probably tracked me to Ramah and are coming to murder me. Please, do something! You're a prophet. Help!"

The aged prophet may have replied, "David, my son, do you think God would choose you out of the sheepfold to let you die at the hands of Saul? You have no idea who you are. Listen to me very carefully. Much more is going on than you know. The Lord has spoken to me very clearly about a plan that He wants you to carry out. He desires night-and-day worship before the ark of the covenant, and He wants you to set it up. It will mirror the worship around the throne in heaven. Just as His throne is the centerpiece of all authority and dominion, when you set up ceaseless worship on the earth, great dominion will be given to you in your kingdom.

When you were on the back side of the desert watching over those sheep and worshiping the Lord, the Lord told me that you were a man after His own heart—one who would do all of His will. This is your destiny. This is who you are!"

I can just imagine David's shock when he first heard the prophetic strategy. The Lord gave him several weeks with Samuel at Ramah in the school of the prophets to help him comprehend God's destiny for his life. Undoubtedly, when the assassins and Saul himself showed up to kill David, and instead began to prophesy, it confirmed to David Samuel's words about his destiny and the tabernacle of worship.

God divinely appointed David's time in Ramah, not only to impart His strategy for the tabernacle, but also to strengthen him in courage. David would spend the next seven years of his life fleeing Saul's fury. The Lord used this strategic meeting to impress upon David's heart the importance of his destiny. In future years, when David would be forced to live in caves and foreign cities, he would need to draw upon the prophetic encounters of his early years for courage to persevere and accomplish all that God had planned.

Ultimately, David would not ascend to the throne over all Israel until he was thirty-seven years old, after both Saul and his heir had died. When David finally became king, the first thing he did was to retake Jerusalem from the Jebusites, who had fortified themselves on top of Mount Zion. After he removed the Jebusites, he retrieved the ark of God and brought it to Jerusalem. In obedience to the Lord's plan, he *immediately* set up night-and-day worship as the central facet of his kingdom, and Israel prospered greatly.

The key to understanding David's life is understanding that from his earliest days his entire life's focus was set on establishing the tabernacle to host the presence of the Lord through night-and-day worship and prayer. From the moment he set up the tabernacle, worship and prayer before the Lord night and day became the blueprint for corporate worship for the people of God throughout Israel's successive generations.

David's life is a testimony to God's desire for night-and-day prayer to be practiced on earth as it is in heaven. In the next chapter, we will examine David's commitment to see night-and-day prayer as the centerpiece of the kingdom of Israel.

Notes

1. 1 Samuel 7.
2. 1 Samuel 25:1.

3

David's Vow

> Lord, remember David
> And all his afflictions;
> How he swore to the Lord,
> And vowed to the Mighty One of Jacob:
> "Surely I will not go into the chamber of my house,
> Or go up to the comfort of my bed;
> I will not give sleep to my eyes
> Or slumber to my eyelids,
> Until I find a place for the Lord,
> A dwelling place for the Mighty One of Jacob."
>
> PSALM 132:1–5

PSALM 132 RECORDS A VOW that David made to see a dwelling place for God established on the earth. It would be a place where God's presence would rest among His people and where His people could encounter Him. This desire was the chief pursuit of David's entire life. And so he fastened himself to it by making a vow.

A biblical vow was a serious matter. One did not take a vow lightly. Vows involved a commitment, not to be departed from under any circumstances. When an individual broke a vow, it was punishable as sin. As Bob Sorge says, "A vow is a resolve on steroids."[1]

Undoubtedly, David was deeply convicted to make such a promise to God. I believe it was in the wake of his encounter with Samuel at Ramah that he made this vow to the Lord. He had heard the words of the prophet. He had seen the sovereign activity

of God. And now his heart burned with a singular vision: to see
the ark of God come back to Israel and a ceaseless expression of
worship established for the glory of His name. It was in this place
of unceasing worship that God's presence would manifest in an
unceasing encounter.

Consider the words of David's vow—"I will not go into the
chamber of my house or go up to the comfort of my bed; I will
not give sleep to my eyes or slumber to my eyelids, until I find a
place for the LORD, a dwelling place for the Mighty One of Jacob."

Was David vowing to never sleep again? Obviously not—that
would be impossible. Instead, his words portray his unrelenting
desire to see a habitation for God's presence established in his
generation.

The Lord had told Samuel, "I have found David, the son of
Jesse, a man after my own heart, who will do all my will." What
was it that made David "a man after God's own heart"? Was it
his perfect actions? No. Reading through the details of David's
life quickly acquaints you with his numerous failures and poor
decisions. Like any of us, he was just a man with a broken nature,
in need of grace.

What then was it that caught God's eye about David? It was his
heart. As a shepherd boy he worshiped while no one was watching.
His hunger for God grew in that secret place, hidden from human
eyes but fully in view of God. It was those days of love on the back
side of Bethlehem that touched God and forever marked David—so
much so, that after David came to power in Israel, though he had
supreme authority over the nation's military and treasury, he still
declared, "One thing I have desired of the LORD, that will I seek,
that I may dwell in the house of the LORD all the days of my life"
(Psalm 27:4).

The first time God mentioned David as a "man after His own
heart" was when Samuel rebuked Saul for not waiting on the Lord
(1 Samuel 13:14). Saul was facing the Philistine armies. Samuel had
given him strict instructions to wait for him to come and make

a sacrifice to the Lord. When Samuel delayed, Saul took matters into his own hands and made the sacrifice himself. At that very moment Samuel returned to find Saul in direct disobedience to the command of the Lord.

Samuel's rebuke was pungent:

> "You have done foolishly. You have not kept the command-ment of the LORD your God, which He commanded you. For now the LORD would have established your kingdom over Israel forever. But now your kingdom shall not continue. The LORD has sought for Himself a man after His own heart, and the LORD has commanded him to be commander over His people, because you have not kept what the LORD commanded you." (1 Samuel 13:13–14)

In this one act of disobedience, Saul's heart was revealed—He valued his reputation more than he revered God. It was this core issue that caused Him to lose favor with the Lord and ultimately be rejected as king.

A Thirteen-Year-Old Captures God's Heart

Many commentators believe that David was approximately thir-teen years old at this time. It's amazing that God had identified a thirteen-year-old boy as the successor to the throne of Israel. What was it about David that had captured God's gaze?

Remember, David had been left to watch the sheep when Samuel had come to town to anoint one of Jesse's sons as king. It speaks volumes that Jesse thought so little of his youngest son that he would leave him to his work while Samuel, this prophet of great renown, visited his house. Apparently, David's own father did not think much of him. Rejected by his father and disdained by his own brothers, David caught the eye of the Lord. What was it about him that caught God's attention?

The answer is simple: David valued the presence of God more

than anything else in his life. At a tender age, while caring for the sheep, he cultivated a deep well of encounter with the Lord. Imagine the nights he spent worshiping the Lord outside the view of any human eye, but fully under the gaze of God. Those endless nights of deep adoration differentiated David from Saul and all the others. He may not have been the most impressive to look at, but his heart was fully given to the Lord. Whereas Saul desired man's praise above all else, David desired God's presence. Saul feared the people and obeyed their voice, but David feared the Lord and obeyed His voice.

David's distinguishing attribute was that he prioritized God's presence above everything else in life. That's what it means to be a man after God's own heart—you want God's presence more than you want anything else. His hunger for God's presence catapulted a forgotten shepherd boy from a forgotten town into the role of king over all Israel. Though he wasn't valued by men, he was chosen by God because of this one outstanding trait.

It is the same with you and me; God is moved by hearts that are moved by Him. It's not our external accomplishments that move God's heart, but an internal hunger for His presence.

Even as I write these words, tears fill my eyes, because ultimately my greatest desire is to be a man who prioritizes God's presence over everything in life. I want to have a heart like that thirteen-year-old boy, who, in desire for intimacy with God, caught heaven's eye. Perhaps you feel the same. Take a moment and pray right now for God to give you a heart like David's, a heart that longs for His presence above everything else.

The Outcome of the Vow

I believe it was after David's encounter with Samuel at Ramah that he made his historic vow found in Psalm 132, a vow that governed David all of His days. Throughout his life, he pursued one singular purpose: to establish a dwelling place for God. But the fulfillment of David's vow wasn't actually realized in his own lifetime. Though he built the tabernacle of David, it was only a precursor to the final fulfillment, the building of the temple of God.

David's son Solomon would ultimately build and dedicate the temple, the resting place for God's presence. The story of the temple's dedication is powerful. Solomon gathered all the elders of the tribes of Israel, along with the Levites and the priests, at a solemn assembly of dedication. When the singers and musicians began to worship with one accord, the glory of the Lord filled the temple. The cloud of glory was so thick that the worshipers could not continue to worship.[2] But that wasn't the end.

With the glory of God resting on the newly built temple, Solomon began to pray. He asked the Lord for continued mercy toward Israel in times of blessing and in future times of waywardness. The final words of his prayer are particularly interesting. They are found in two places in the Bible, 2 Chronicles 6 and Psalm 132.

"Now therefore, arise, O LORD God, to Your resting place, You and the ark of Your strength. Let Your priests, O LORD God, be clothed with salvation, and let Your saints rejoice in goodness. O LORD God, do not turn away the face of Your Anointed; remember the mercies of Your servant David." (2 Chronicles 6:41–42)

Arise, O LORD, to Your resting place, You and the ark of Your strength. Let Your priests be clothed with righteousness, and let Your saints shout for joy. For Your servant David's sake, do not turn away the face of Your Anointed. (Psalm 132:8–10)

The words from Psalm 132 were first spoken by Solomon at the dedication of the temple. When we think about the whole of Psalm 132 we see that Solomon was calling into remembrance David's vow, and asking God to answer David's heart cry to establish a dwelling place for God.

The conclusion was incredible.

"When Solomon had finished praying, fire came down from heaven and consumed the burnt offering and the sacrifices, and the glory of the Lord filled the temple. And the priests could not enter the house of the Lord, because the glory of the Lord had filled the Lord's house. When all the children of Israel saw how the fire came down, and the glory of the Lord on the temple, they bowed their faces to the ground on the pavement, and worshiped and praised the Lord, saying: 'For He is good, for His mercy endures forever.'" (2 Chronicles 7:1–3)

What began in the heart of a thirteen-year-old boy as a hunger for the presence of God culminated in heavenly fire falling and the glory of God being manifested. The entire nation was ultimately impacted by the deep desire of that young man.

God is right now calling forth an entire generation in the same vein as David, who will give themselves to aggressive pursuit of His presence above all else. He's looking for a people who will seek Him with all their heart, mind, soul, and strength. And He aims to bring the same result in this day as He did in David's—the manifestation of His glory on the earth. Except this time, rather than His glory filling a single temple, He's going to cover the earth with glory as the waters cover the sea.[3]

If the vow that David made resonates in your heart, it is the Lord's doing. People don't desire the Lord in that way unless He initiates it. I encourage you to ask the Lord for grace to spend your days seeking Him until His presence breaks out in your church and city. Oh Lord, let your presence and power fill our churches the way it filled the temple, in Solomon's day.

Notes

1. Bob Sorge, *A Covenant with My Eyes* (Grandview, MO: Oasis House, 2013), 87.
2. 2 Chronicles 5:15.
3. Habakkuk 2:14; cf. Isaiah 6:3.

$$4$$

Old Testament Accounts of Night-and-Day Prayer

N OW THAT WE UNDERSTAND A little bit of God's dealings with David, let's consider the history of night-and-day prayer throughout the Old Testament. David's tabernacle is by no means the only account of night-and-day prayer in the Bible, but it is the first. David's tabernacle became the model for ceaseless worship, which was used throughout subsequent generations in Israel up to the time of Jesus. Though David set the standard for night-and-day prayer, the idea of ceaseless worship actually originated with Moses.

In the days of the exodus from Egypt, about one thousand years before David's tabernacle, God directed Moses to build a tabernacle in the wilderness so that Israel could worship Him. He gave Moses very specific instructions regarding its construction, as well as regulations for the order of worship. The writer of Hebrews tells us that this tabernacle and the order of worship were symbolic of the heavenly worship that takes place before the throne of God.[1]

One of the most interesting features of Moses' tabernacle was the burnt offering that was offered to the Lord every morning and every evening.[2] The burnt offering was to be a one-year-old lamb without spot or blemish, and was to be sacrificed by the priest and offered upon the altar. The fire upon the altar was to never go out, aflame all day and all night.[3] God wanted it to stay lit to signify continual worship and devotion from His people.

The first account we have of the high priest offering the daily burnt offering is found in Leviticus 9. After Aaron had been consecrated to the Lord and set apart to his priestly office, he was to offer a burnt offering to the Lord. Having offered this and several other offerings, he and his brother, Moses, blessed the people, and the glory of the Lord appeared before the whole congregation. In a moment, heavenly fire exploded from the presence of the Lord and consumed the burnt offering.

Can you imagine the sight of the glory of God appearing in plain view to over two million people? The flash of God's fire was so powerful that all the people shouted and fell on their faces; the altar was set ablaze with heavenly glory.[4] This consuming fire continued to burn night and day upon the altar throughout Israel's sojourn in the wilderness. The priests fueled it morning and night with fresh wood, removing the ashes from the previous day's sacrifice and offering anew another lamb.[5]

This fire was symbolic of the continual devotion that God desires from His people. God was the One who supplied the heavenly fire, but it was the priests' responsibility to make sure it was kept burning by continuing to offer daily sacrifices to the Lord. The offering was a sweet aroma to the Lord.[6]

In this same manner, the Lord ignites our hearts with His holy fire. And like the priests of old, it is our responsibility to make sure that we continually offer our hearts to Him in worship and adoration to keep the fire of God burning brightly within us.

It was this template of ceaseless worship that provided the backdrop for David's tabernacle.

Tabernacle of David, 1050 BC

So he left Asaph and his relatives there before the ark of the covenant of the LORD *to minister before the ark continually*, as every day's work required. (1 Chronicles 16:37, NASB)

It was David who first understood that the Lord longed for hearts that would continually offer Him worship and praise. He understood that worship and praise from a sincere heart would bless the Lord more than burnt offerings and sacrifices.[7] David's heart of love and devotion to the Lord caused him to establish a new order of worship in Israel.

In approximately 1050 BC, David set up a tent in Jerusalem where night-and-day worship with singers and musicians took place before the ark of God. This tent was called the tabernacle of David. This new order of worship was *in addition to* the offerings that were still being offered to the Lord in the tabernacle of Moses at Gibeon. These two expressions of worship continued to operate simultaneously throughout the entirety of David's reign. David kept both forms of worship side by side, because he understood that one was symbolic of the other—the fire that burned perpetually on the altar in the tabernacle of Moses was a symbol of the night-and-day worship taking place in the tabernacle of David.

God longs to be continually intimate with His people. He wants to engage with His people twenty-four hours a day. And He wants the hearts of His people to burn constantly with His passion and fire. Thus, David's tabernacle continued in ceaseless worship and adoration to the Lord in answer to God's desire for perpetual intimacy with His people.

The tabernacle of David employed 288 Levites who were gifted in singing the prophetic songs of the Lord, and who were organized into twenty-four teams, each with twelve members.[8] This group of gifted singers led a larger group of musicians that eventually grew to four thousand. They used instruments that David designed himself.[9] Another four thousand gatekeepers took care of the service of the tabernacle. Altogether, over eight thousand Levites were employed full-time to offer night-and-day worship and praise before the ark of the Lord. It was in this context that David wrote the majority of his psalms.

Immediately after David set up night-and-day prayer, the Lord gave him two amazing promises. First, He promised David that He would give him dominion and establish his house forever. This meant that there would never cease to be a king from David's family line ruling upon the throne of Israel. The second promise was even more astounding. God promised David that the Messiah would come from this line of kings. In other words, Messiah would be a "son of David."[10]

God gave these promises to David as a direct result of David's desire to establish night-and-day prayer. The promise of dominion was not only a reality throughout David's life, but also for every king of Judah who established night-and-day prayer under his own leadership.

Six other kings of Judah established night-and-day prayer according to the Davidic model, and each of them experienced seasons of blessing and revival. When a king did not uphold the Davidic order of worship, the kingdom would begin to fall into disarray and the people would give themselves to idol worship.

Solomon, 1010 BC

And, *according to the order of David* his father, he appointed the divisions of the priests for their service . . . for so David the man of God had commanded. (2 Chronicles 8:14)

In approximately 1010 BC, Solomon, David's son, completed the temple of the Lord in Jerusalem. Solomon commanded that the temple worship should be in accordance with the Davidic order.[11] In the temple, Solomon combined night-and-day worship from the tabernacle of David with the sacrificial system from the tabernacle of Moses. At the dedication of the temple, the glory of the Lord appeared with such power that the priests could not stand to minister.[12] This powerful manifestation of God's presence testified of the Lord's approval of the temple and the ministry of night-and-day worship, as well as His pleasure toward His people.

During Solomon's reign, there was great favor upon Israel, and God's presence and blessing were continually manifest among the people. During his reign, the Lord appeared to Solomon on two different occasions. On the first, the Lord said to Solomon, "Ask! What shall I give you?" Solomon asked for wisdom, and the Lord endowed Him with more wisdom than anyone who had ever lived. With his God-given understanding, Solomon made decisions that caused the kingdom of Israel to multiply in greatness. The people were so financially prosperous that silver was considered common and not even valuable during Solomon's reign.[13]

The dominion that the Lord promised David was manifest during the reign of Solomon. God exalted Israel in an unprecedented way, and the nation experienced unprecedented peace and prosperity. Unfortunately, this prosperity and blessing did not last. In Solomon's later years, he turned away from the Lord and began to worship the gods of his foreign wives. Because of this tragic mistake, the kingdom was divided and the people went into years of backsliding and idolatry.

Joash and Jehoiada, 853 BC

Also Jehoiada appointed the oversight of the house of the LORD to the hand of the priests, the Levites, whom David had assigned in the house of the LORD . . . with rejoicing and with singing, *as it was established* by David. (2 Chronicles 23:18)

After the reign of Solomon, the kingdom was divided. Ten of the tribes of Israel split and moved to the north, making Tirzah their capital, and later Samaria, while two tribes remained in the south, with their capital in Jerusalem. The northern kingdom never served the Lord. The southern went through seasons of backsliding and revival, depending upon the leadership of the current king.

Approximately 125 years after Solomon's reign, Jehoshaphat, a righteous king, ascended to the throne of the southern kingdom. However, the years following his reign were dark times for the kingdom of Judah. Though Jehoshaphat had served the Lord with all his heart, he made a fatal political error. In an effort to bring peace between the northern and the southern kingdoms, he agreed to give his son Jehoram in marriage to Athaliah,[14] the daughter of Ahab and Jezebel, the wicked monarchs of the north. Ahab and Jezebel had led the entire nation of Israel to worship Baal, and their daughter was no different.

After Jehoram died, his son Ahaziah ruled Judah. His reign was cut short by Jehu, who had been anointed to destroy all from the lineage of Ahab.[15] When Jehu killed Ahaziah only one year into his reign, Ahaziah's mother, Athaliah, seized the throne. Her lust for power and her wicked ambition drove her to kill all of her grandsons. She wanted to blot out the royal seed so that she could rule Judah as queen.

Her plan succeeded, except for one point. Jehosheba hid Joash, Athaliah's grandson, in the temple of the Lord under the care of the priest Jehoiada for six years. And for six years Athaliah reigned in Judah, spreading her wickedness and Baal worship throughout the kingdom. But when Joash was seven years old, Jehoiada the priest made a covenant with the military commanders to restore Joash, the rightful heir, to the throne. The commanders of the military killed Athaliah, and made Joash, a descendant of the line of David, king in her place. The people rejoiced and the city was at peace, having been delivered from Athaliah's wicked ways.[16]

Joash cleansed and restored the temple. He reinstituted the practice of giving offerings to the priests to provide for their living expenses so that they could freely serve the Lord in the temple. Athaliah's sons had desecrated the temple, so Joash commanded that the offerings he collected be used to restore the temple and reinstate the priesthood. Joash, under the guidance of Jehoiada the priest, also reinstated the temple service with the daily burnt offerings and the Davidic order of night-and-day worship.[17] Under his leadership the people of Judah tore down the temple of Baal and killed its priest. The nation experienced a season of revival as the people turned away from Baal worship and gave themselves in abandonment to the Lord.[18] The restoration of the daily offerings and night-and-day worship led to this season of renewal in Judah.

Hezekiah, 726 BC

> He stationed the Levites in the house of the LORD with cymbals, with stringed instruments, and with harps, *according to the commandment of David.* (2 Chronicles 29:25)

One hundred twenty-five years after Joash, Hezekiah ruled in Judah. He was the son of Ahaz, a very wicked king, who had encouraged moral decline in Judah and had rebelled against the Lord. Ahaz had offered sacrifices to the gods of the nations that had defeated him in battle; he had discontinued the worship of the Lord in the temple, actually shutting up the doors of the temple so that no one could enter. He had taken the holy articles from the temple and cut them into pieces, and set up altars to false gods in every town of Judah, provoking the Lord to anger. Because of him, the Lord had allowed Judah to be conquered by Syria.[19]

When Hezekiah became king, he realized that Judah and Jerusalem's problems were due to their abandonment of the Lord and their worship of false gods. So he set out to reform the kingdom. As soon as he took the throne, he reopened the temple and had the priests work to restore everything that had been destroyed. He again employed the Levites in offering the daily sacrifices and practicing night-and-day worship according to the order of David. He called the *entire* nation of Israel, from the northern and southern kingdoms, to come and celebrate the Passover feast. The people returned to the Lord under his leadership, and Judah prospered greatly. The nation had not experienced the blessing of the Lord in this manner since the days of Solomon.

During the reign of Hezekiah, the king of Assyria attempted to besiege Jerusalem and take the people captive. Twenty years earlier, Assyria had invaded and destroyed the northern kingdom of Israel. Now the southern kingdom was under siege. The Lord told Hezekiah to resist the Assyrian king and to cry out to the Lord for deliverance. In one night, the angel of the Lord destroyed 185,000 soldiers from the Assyrian army, bringing a stunning victory and deliverance to Hezekiah and the people of Judah.[20] Perhaps only when the Lord delivered Israel from Egypt had Israel ever experienced such a powerful deliverance from her enemies.

When Hezekiah reopened the temple, reinstituted the daily sacrifices, and re-established the Davidic order of worship, the Lord began to bless the nation in an incredible way. National repentance and revival broke out among the people. The Lord caused the nation to turn back to Him. He greatly prospered them and once again gave them dominion—just as He had promised David. As long as night-and-day prayer was the centerpiece of the nation, God brought great blessing, power, and deliverance to His people.

Josiah, 635 BC

The singers, the sons of Asaph, were in their places, *according to the command of David.* (2 Chronicles 35:15)

After Hezekiah died, his son Manasseh ruled for fifty-five years in Judah. Manasseh did not follow the ways of the Lord, but instead led the people into extreme wickedness. He rebuilt the altars to the false gods that his father had destroyed, and he set up idols in the house of the Lord.

Later in life, Manasseh humbled himself before God and turned back to the Lord, but the nation had gone terribly astray. His son

Amon ruled after him and committed the same sins that he had. When Amon was murdered, his son Josiah took the throne.

Josiah was eight years old when he became king in Jerusalem. He aggressively pursued the Lord, and by the time he was twenty years old he began tearing down all the altars to false gods that had been set up throughout Judah. Soon, he had thoroughly purged the land by destroying all the high places and altars used to worship false gods.

During his reign, the priests found the book of the law of Moses, which had been lost, and they read it to Josiah. When he heard the words of the Lord he knew that the nation was in danger of judgment, for the people had departed from the ways of the Lord. Josiah wept and repented on behalf of the people. The Lord answered him and told him that though judgment was indeed coming, He was going to give the people a season of clemency. He reassured Josiah that as long as he was alive, the Lord would not release the appointed judgment upon the people.[21]

Josiah reestablished the Passover, as his great-grandfather Hezekiah had done. He also reinstituted the Davidic order of worship in the service of the temple.[22] Josiah's reforms brought about a season of revival and the release of the mercy of the Lord to Judah. When the people turned to the Lord, and while the Levites practiced night-and-day worship, the nation prospered greatly.

Zerubbabel, 538 BC

When the builders laid the foundation of the temple of the LORD, the priests stood in their apparel with trumpets, and the Levites, the sons of Asaph, with cymbals, to praise the LORD, *according to the ordinance of David king of Israel.* (Ezra 3:10–13)

After years of backsliding in Israel, in 606 BC, the Babylonian army swept down upon Jerusalem, destroying the temple, burning the city, and taking the remnant of Israel captive. God allowed this to happen because His people had once again turned away from Him and disregarded His ways. God raised up the nation of Babylon as an instrument of His judgment, but prophesied through Jeremiah that after seventy years the people would be released from their captivity and return to Jerusalem[23].

After sixty-nine years of Israel's captivity in Babylon, Daniel, having understood the prophecies of Jeremiah, cried out to the Lord to keep His word and deliver God's people from captivity. God was true to His promise. In 536 BC, exactly seventy years after the Babylonian invasion, He stirred up the heart of the Persian king, Cyrus, to release the Jewish captives so that they could return to Jerusalem and rebuild the temple of the Lord.[24] Cyrus commissioned all who desired to return to complete the task of rebuilding the temple.

Approximately fifty thousand Jews returned to Jerusalem, traveling hundreds of miles across the desert on foot to rebuild the house of the Lord. Once the foundation was laid, the singers and Levites were commissioned to reestablish night-and-day worship according to the order of David.

They understood that the Lord desired more than just a building—He longed for a people who would pursue Him continuously, worshiping and adoring His name. As long as the people practiced night-and-day worship, they prospered; but when they lost their focus, they faltered. Clearly, night-and-day worship and prayer was one of the Lord's central purposes in bringing His people out of captivity.

Nehemiah, 446 BC

Both the singers and the gatekeepers kept the charge of their God and the charge of the purification, *according to the command of David* and Solomon his son. For in the days of David and Asaph of old there were chiefs of the singers, and songs of praise and thanksgiving to God. In the days of Zerubbabel and in the days of Nehemiah all Israel gave the portions for the singers and the gatekeepers, a portion for each day. They also consecrated holy things for the Levites, and the Levites consecrated them for the children of Aaron. (Nehemiah 12:45–47)

About seventy years after the temple was rebuilt, the Lord stirred Nehemiah, who was a Jew still living in Babylon, to move to his homeland and oversee the rebuilding of the wall surrounding Jerusalem. He had heard that Jerusalem was in great distress and that the wall around the city still lay in disrepair.[25] Nehemiah was a trusted servant, the cupbearer to Artaxerxes, king of Persia. When he explained to the king that his heart was deeply grieved because of the condition of his people and his nation, the king granted his request, allowing him to go to Jerusalem to assess the state of his people and to offer aid.

When Nehemiah arrived, what he beheld justified the burden upon his heart. The people were greatly disheartened and the wall was in ruins, with its gates having been burned to the ground some ninety years earlier. The city was without protection from neighboring nations. Were it not for the protection of Persia, marauding raiders would have once again ransacked Jerusalem.

Upon Nehemiah's arrival, he quickly rallied some of the leaders and put together a plan to rebuild the wall around the city. The neighboring nations had been extremely hostile toward the Jews and did not want to see them prosper. Amidst much opposition from the other nations, Nehemiah led the Jews in rebuilding the wall in only fifty-two days[26].

Though the temple had been rebuilt in the time of Zerubbabel, the Jews had been negligent in providing for the Levites so that they could be employed in the service of night-and-day prayer. This troubled Nehemiah greatly. Immediately after the wall was completed, Nehemiah, filled with the zeal of the Lord, appointed gatekeepers, singers, and Levites to reinstitute the practice of night-and-day worship.[27] He made sure that the nation continued to provide for the Levites so that night-and-day prayer continued during his lifetime.[28]

Malachi's Prophecy

"From the rising of the sun, even to its going down, My name shall be great among the Gentiles; in every place incense shall be offered to My name, and a pure offering: for My name shall be great among the nations," says the LORD of hosts. (Malachi 1:11)

The prophet Malachi was a contemporary of Nehemiah. Because of Israel's apathy toward the Lord, God raised up Malachi to rebuke the wayward nation, calling them back to righteousness. Malachi described in detail a shift in God's plan for night-and-day worship. He said that one day the temple would no longer be the only place of ceaseless worship—instead, the Lord's praises would fill Gentile nations throughout the earth. This was unthinkable to the Jews at that time. How could it be that Gentiles would engage in continuous adoration of Jehovah?

Malachi's prophecies proclaimed a transition from God's dwelling being solely among the nation of Israel to being among people from all nations. In essence, the Lord was saying through Malachi, "Because you have neglected Me in regard to My desire for intimacy with you, I am going to provoke you to jealousy by inviting the Gentiles into intimacy with Me."

Night-and-day prayer was always supposed to be the center-piece of the corporate worship experience for God's people through-out every generation. Every king who instituted night-and-day worship and prayer experienced seasons of revival and blessing. But those who neglected it went astray and worshiped idols, hence bringing God's disfavor and judgment upon themselves and the nation. God desired night-and-day worship and prayer to be the centerpiece of worship and governance for the nation of Israel. We will see in the next chapter how night-and-day worship and prayer was not only for Israel, but is also for God's people in every generation, even throughout the age to come.

Notes

1. Hebrews 9:1–12.
2. Exodus 29:38–42.
3. Leviticus 6:13.
4. Leviticus 9:23–24.
5. Leviticus 6:12–13.
6. Exodus 29:41.
7. Psalm 69:30–31.
8. 1 Chronicles 25:7–31.
9. 1 Chronicles 23:5.
10. 2 Samuel 7:8–16.
11. 2 Chronicles 8:14–15.
12. 2 Chronicles 5:14; 7:1–3.
13. 1 Kings 10:21.
14. 2 Kings 8:16–18, 26.
15. 2 Kings 9:6–8.
16. 2 Kings 11.
17. 2 Chronicles 23:16–18.
18. 2 Kings 12.
19. 2 Chronicles 28:5.
20. 2 Chronicles 32.
21. 2 Chronicles 34:23–28.
22. 2 Chronicles 35:3–4.
23. Jeremiah 25:11–12; 29:10.
24. Ezra 1:1–2.
25. Nehemiah 1:3.
26. Nehemiah 6:15.
27. Nehemiah 7:1.
28. Nehemiah 12–13.

5

My House Shall Be Called a House of Prayer

And He said to them, "It is written, 'My house shall be called a house of prayer,' but you have made it a 'den of thieves.'"

MATTHEW 21:13

WHEN JESUS ENTERED THE TEMPLE, nearly five hundred years after Nehemiah, He was angered when He saw moneychangers buying and selling in the temple courts. The moneychangers were using the Passover as an opportunity to profit by changing the currency of the pilgrims coming to the feast at exorbitant rates. The powerful rebuke that Jesus leveled against them made clear the principle issue upon his heart—He burned with desire for night-and-day worship.

The priests had accommodated those who were greedy for financial gain, allowing them to practice their "trade" in the courts of the Lord. At the same time, they were neglecting the intimacy of true worship and prayer that the Lord so deeply desired. Even though daily sacrifices continued to be offered in the temple, the practice had become a mere ritual, lacking any true intimacy between the people and their God.

Jesus had walked into these very temple courts three years earlier and driven out the same moneychangers with a whip.[2] Here, now at the end of His life, He once again zealously confronted those who were commercializing and capitalizing on the feast of the Lord. Nowhere else in the gospels does Jesus physically engage with people to obstruct them from their sin, but this time it was different. Burning with zeal, He drove out all who obstructed God's desire for a pure offering from His people.

Jesus inaugurated and finalized His ministry by cleansing the temple. These two acts are bookends of His earthly ministry. What compelled Him to accentuate His ministry in this way? His piercing proclamation, "My house shall be called a house of prayer." When Jesus made this declaration, it was as if He was saying, "Where is the prayer? You know that My Father has always dreamed of continual worship and intimacy with His people. How could you replace the very thing my Father's heart longs for with commerce and greed?"

But His words fell on deaf ears. Only a few days later, the nation of Israel would crucify her King, putting Him to death in the same way common criminals were executed. Within forty years, Jerusalem and her temple would be besieged and destroyed, this time by the Roman army. The Jews had exchanged their devotion to God for financial gain and religious ritual—all to their demise.

Jesus' words not only served as a correction for the people of His day, they serve as a prophetic declaration of God's intention for His house in every generation: "My house shall be called a house of prayer." This is a broad statement, indicating the prescribed culture the people of God are to practice. God's desire for His church was that they would be so given to prayer that they would be known by this distinguishing characteristic above all else. He could have defined many other things as the key identifier for His house: a house of teaching, a house of evangelism, a house of salvation. Yet He chose a house of prayer. It's because all the activity of the kingdom is to be initiated, maintained, and accomplished through the vehicle of prayer. In fact nothing of kingdom value is ever accomplished apart from the governance of prayer.

Jesus is looking for a people who will love Him ceaselessly and involve Him continually in everything they desire to do in the kingdom. He is looking for a culture of prayer that will pervade the community of faith.

I'm not suggesting that every individual church operate in 24/7 worship and prayer. I do believe, however, that much can be gained if we consider Jesus' words along with the biblical precedent, and honestly ask how we may carry out His desires in our churches, individually and across our cities.

Could it be, in the church today, that we too have exchanged simple intimacy with God for seeking prosperity and man's praise? Perhaps we have become mired in the same sins that seduced first-century Israel. We must remember that rather than bringing financial prosperity and blessing, Israel's departure from intimacy with God and negligence regarding night-and-day prayer resulted in her ultimate destruction.

Jesus' Call for Night-and-Day Worship

While we consider Jesus' call for night-and-day worship, it is important to note the context of the Old Testament passage he was quoting from. Isaiah first declared the phrase, "My house shall be called a house of prayer for all nations."[3] Isaiah 56 speaks of a future time, when God's salvation will be fully manifest and His righteousness completely revealed throughout the nations of the earth.[4] This will take place in the age to come, when Jesus Himself will reign from Jerusalem. In that day, people from all nations will journey to Jerusalem to worship the Lord.[5] The ultimate fulfillment of the temple becoming a house of prayer for all nations is actually reserved for this future time.

When the temple was still standing, only Jews were allowed to enter—Gentiles were not admitted beyond the court of the Gentiles. In the age to come, however, worshipers from all nations—male and female, Jew and Gentile—will be drawn to Jerusalem and admitted into the temple to praise and glorify Jesus.

By quoting Isaiah's prophecy, Jesus was pointing ahead to this future time. He was proclaiming the far-reaching vision of God concerning His house of prayer. In so doing, He was tying together God's future purposes with His plan for night-and-day prayer in this age. *The temple was always intended to function as an international house of prayer.* God never changed the corporate worship design for the people of God. He never revoked His command to Moses: "The fire on the altar shall be kept burning on it; it shall not be put out."[6] It's important to note that the very centerpiece of kingdom culture and the corporate worship expression for God's people has always been night-and-day worship and prayer, and it will continue to be in the age to come. Could it be that Jesus was pointing to this future reality to express that continuous worship and prayer should also be embraced and practiced in this age?

Night-and-Day Worship in the Age to Come

Amos prophesied of a future day when the tabernacle of David would be rebuilt.[7] Isaiah prophesied that Jesus would rule upon a throne in the rebuilt tabernacle of David.[8] Zechariah proclaimed that Jesus would be a priest, ruling from a throne in the temple.[9] None of these prophecies have yet come to pass, but all of them describe the day when Jesus will return to rule the nations and establish His reign on the earth in Jerusalem. He will rule from the rebuilt tabernacle of David, with night-and-day worship and prayer taking place before His throne.

In heaven, worship choruses continue before the Father's throne unceasingly. The twenty-four elders and the living creatures, along with a myriad of angels and saints, worship the Lord in perpetual perfection. The heavenly throne room is ablaze with beauty and sound. It operates as an eternal night-and-day worship sanctuary.[10] When Jesus returns, He will set up His throne on the earth as a mirror of the Father's throne in heaven. Day-and-night prayer and worship will be offered to the Lord on the earth as it is in heaven. Imagine that day, when all nations will come and bow down in worship and adoration before the Lord Jesus Himself. This is our destiny and God's ultimate plan for the general worship assembly of His people in the age to come.

The Common Thread

Night-and-day worship and prayer is a consistent thread weaving together the Old and New Testaments, as well as the age to come. Is it possible that we have overlooked this central facet of biblical worship? The apostles were well aware of the essential nature of the tabernacle of David. In the Jerusalem council, they quoted Amos' prophecy speaking of the day the tabernacle would be rebuilt and serve as a light to the Gentile nations.[11] They identified the standard of unity in worship in the tabernacle of David as an essential facet for unity between Jew and Gentile believers under the new covenant.

The fact that James, the leader of the council, chose to quote from the prophecy of Amos is significant. There are many Old Testament verses James could have referenced to illustrate the Gentiles' participation in the kingdom of God. However, he intentionally selected a verse that describes the reestablishment of the tabernacle of David. This implies that the apostles considered the vision for night-and-day prayer not only to be an Old Testament phenomenon, but also a New Testament reality.

Let's not forget that David, the greatest psalmist in the Bible, wrote the majority of his psalms in the context of night-and-day worship and prayer. Furthermore, the throne room in heaven is a place of continuous worship and praise. Shouldn't the community of faith in some way resemble this heavenly pattern?

Final Considerations

As we consider the place for night-and-day worship and prayer in our day, it is important to ask ourselves a few questions. For instance: Was there ever a time when the Lord instructed His people to stop worshiping Him night and day? Is there any admonition

against night-and-day worship? As I began to personally investigate these, I found quite the contrary. Not only is there biblical
precedent for night-and-day worship and prayer, but there are
actually biblical commands for God's people to practice it. Consider
this passage describing Hezekiah's reformation, "And he stationed
the Levites in the house of the Lord with cymbals, with stringed
instruments, and with harps, according to the commandment of
David, of Gad the king's seer, and of Nathan the prophet; for *thus
was the commandment of the Lord by his prophets*" (2 Chronicles
29:25). It's notable that Hezekiah, who lived approximately 275 years
after David, was treating the commands of the prophets during
David's time as applicable to his generation.

Is it possible that we, like the nation of Israel, have neglected
the very thing that the Lord always desired—a never-ending expression of worship from His beloved?

Some may argue that in the new covenant, individual believers
are the temple of the Holy Spirit, and we no longer need a corporate expression of ceaseless worship. While it is true that believers
are the temple of the Holy Spirit, we must also consider the truth
that the corporate expression of worship throughout Scripture
was always centered around night-and-day worship and prayer.

Under the old covenant, unceasing worship was a symbol and
prophetic picture of the abiding intimacy that the Lord desires
with His people, both corporately and individually. Though the
veil of the temple is now rent and the Spirit of God indwells believers, this in no way cancels God's desire for ceaseless worship
gatherings. Rather than replacing it, the indwelling Spirit testifies
of and affirms the Lord's desire to continuously dwell among His
people in power.

In the new covenant we are individually temples of the Holy
Spirit, yet at the same time, we are being built *together* as a dwelling
place for God.[11] I believe there is much available for the church if we
will make room for the habitation of God in our midst. He dwells
within each of us individually but He still longs for a perpetual

dwelling place among His people. Perhaps a people embracing a culture of perpetual worship and prayer is at least in part the answer to the Father's question, "Where is the house that you will build for Me?" (Isaiah 66:1).

Notes

1. John 2:15–16.
2. Isaiah 56:7.
3. Isaiah 56:1.
4. Psalm 86:9; Isaiah 2:2; 66:18; Haggai 2:7; Zechariah 14:16.
5. Leviticus 6:12.
6. Amos 9:11–15.
7. Isaiah 16:5.
8. Zechariah 6:12–13.
9. Revelation 4:8.
10. Acts 15:16–17.
11. Ephesians 2:22.

Historical Accounts of Night-and-Day Prayer

NIGHT-AND-DAY PRAYER MAY BE CONSIDERED a relatively new or recent trend in the body of Christ. However, there are multiple examples of communities of believers throughout church history who have practiced night-and-day prayer.

The earliest post-biblical examples are found in monastic communities. For over one thousand years monasticism held a key role in shaping theology in the church. As early as the fourth century, monks and nuns were regarded as an integral part of society throughout the developing world. The early monastic communities coined the phrase *laus perennis*, or perpetual prayer. Through the monastic tradition, night-and-day prayer was birthed in the church age.

Some of the key figures instrumental in establishing the foundations of modern night-and-day prayer were Alexander Akimetes the Sleepless, Comgall, and Count Ludwig von Zinzendorf. In this chapter we will take a brief look at the lives of these and others who were the pioneers of night-and-day prayer as we know it.

Alexander the Sleepless, AD 400

Alexander the Sleepless was born in the late fourth century AD to a wealthy family. Having been educated in Constantinople, he enjoyed a short but successful career as a civil servant. One day while studying Scripture he was pierced by Jesus' words to the rich young ruler: "Sell whatever you have and give to the poor, and you will have treasure in heaven; and come, take up the cross, and follow Me" (Mark 10:21). In obedience to the word of the Lord, he sold all that he had, retired from public service, and spent the next several years of his life in solitude in the desert of Syria.

After seven years of solitude, he reappeared and settled on the banks of the Euphrates River. Tradition states that he set fire to a pagan temple and was immediately arrested and thrown into prison. While imprisoned, Alexander led the prison governor and his household to the Lord.

Following his release he converted a band of robbers into devoted Christians. His converts became the core of his new monastic movement. He began to gather men to engage in daily singing and chanting of the Scriptures.

Around AD 400, Alexander and approximately fifty of his monks moved to Constantinople, where he had been educated earlier in life. In response to Paul's command to "pray without ceasing" (1 Thessalonians 5:17), Alexander established *laus perennis* in the monastery of Saint Mennas. Over three hundred monks joined him there.

The order, after encountering persecution in Constantinople, relocated to Gomon, at the mouth of the Black Sea, near modern-day Istanbul. In Gomon, Alexander founded the monastic order of the Acoemetae, which is literally translated "the sleepless ones." He divided the monks into six choirs trained to sing continuously in four-hour shifts, and each choir was responsible for a daily four-hour shift. The uninterrupted prayer and worship continued twenty-four hours a day.

There, "Alexander disputed with heretics, worked miracles by the Grace of God, [and] grew old serving the Lord."[1] Alexander died in AD 430, but the influence of the Acoemetae and laus perennis continued for generations.

The most famous monastery to practice laus perennis was Studion, established in Constantinople between 462 and 463 BC.

Studion became a center for education and holiness in the entire region, having night-and-day prayer as its central focus.[2]

The Monastery of Saint Maurice, AD 522

The practice of laus perennis found its way to the Western church in AD 522 through the monastery of Saint Maurice in Agaunum, Switzerland. In AD 286, a Roman legion of around seven thousand Egyptian soldiers under the command of Maurice de Valois was called to assist Emperor Maximian in suppressing a rebellion in Gaul (France). Legend has it that all of the soldiers under Maurice's command were Christians. On their way to Gaul (in Western Europe), Maurice's legion camped at Agaunum. The Roman authorities ordered them to offer a sacrifice to the Roman gods and to the emperor in petition for victory. When they refused, Maximian ordered the execution of the entire legion. All seven thousand Egyptian Christians were martyred because they would not worship the Roman emperor and his false gods.[3]

The legend of the Agaunum martyrs spread, though the accuracy of the story was questioned, and some years later a monastery was established there in memory of the sacrifice of Maurice's legion. Between AD 515 and 521, King Sigismund of Burgundy (a province of eastern and central France) gave a large sum of money to the monastery in order to ensure its success. In AD 522, the abbey of Saint Maurice instituted laus perennis after the tradition of the Acoemetae.[4] Choirs of monks took turns in singing duties day and night, and this practice continued until around AD 900, influencing monasteries all over France and Switzerland.[5]

Saint Patrick and the Vale of Angels

In AD 433, Saint Patrick journeyed to Ireland to preach the gospel. He was followed by others who established monastic centers throughout Ireland. In much of the deteriorating Roman Empire, Christianity had been organized with bishops overseeing cities and metropolitan areas. However, Ireland had never been conquered by Rome and had no urban centers. Thus the church in Ireland was unaffected by the eventual fall of the Roman Empire, and monasteries soon became the primary influence upon Irish society.

According to the twelfth-century monk Jocelin, Patrick once rested in a valley in Bangor, Ireland, where he and his friends saw a vision of heaven. Jocelin wrote, "They held the valley filled with heavenly light, and with a multitude of heaven, they heard, as chanted forth from the voice of angels, the psalmody of the celestial choir."[6] The place became known as the Vallis Angelorum, the Vale of Angels. About a hundred years later, a renowned monastery would be built there that would embrace laus perennis and greatly impact all of Europe.

Comgall and Bangor Monastery, AD 552

Comgall, the man who founded the monastery in Bangor, was born in Ulster, Ireland, in AD 517. Initially he was a soldier, but upon his release from the military he took monastic vows and was educated for his new life as a monk. Comgall's presiding bishop encouraged him to plant a monastery in the famed Vale of Angels. He founded the abbey at Bangor between AD 552 and 559. It is interesting to note that the monastery at Bangor was not Roman Catholic, but Celtic Christian, so it was not presided over by the Roman Catholic diocese and did not practice Catholic traditions.

At Bangor, Comgall instituted a rigid monastic rule of constant prayer and fasting, which attracted rather than repelling the masses. Nearly three thousand monks flocked to Bangor in order to experience Comgall's intensely focused spiritual leadership.[7] The monks of Bangor were divided into seven choirs of 300 monks each, praying in succession throughout the day and night.In this way, prayer and worship continued twenty-four hours a day, with the choirs' singing reminiscent of Saint Patrick's vision of the heavenly choir some 120 years earlier.

Bangor Abbey became the epicenter of spiritual revival and

education in Europe for the next three hundred years. God's power was mightily displayed through the ministry of Comgall.[8] History records that he performed miraculous signs, wonders, and healings, and on one occasion caused blindness to fall on a gang of thieves.[9]

The Monastery of Cluny, AD 910

The ninth and tenth centuries were difficult times throughout Europe. The Vikings were ravaging Europe. Feudalism was on the rise. Monasteries were raided and subjugated by local chieftains. The Clunaic order was not only a reaction to these troubles, but was also one of the most crucial reforms in the European church.

William the Pious, Duke of Aquitaine, founded the monastery at Cluny in AD 910. He installed a man named Berno as the first abbot. William the Pious donated many of his personal resources, as well as his hunting preserve in the forests of Burgundy, to the monastery. This large endowment of resources allowed the abbey to be free from all secular financial and legislative entanglements. This autonomy enabled the monks to commit themselves to laus perennis.[10]

The second abbot, Odo, took over around AD 926. He was zealous to see spiritual reformation touch not only the monastic orders but also the entire society of Europe, and under his leadership that is exactly what happened.[11] Many smaller monastic houses that looked to Cluny as their motherhouse sprouted up throughout the land. Known for its independence, hospitality, and alms giving, the monastery at Cluny removed manual labor from a monk's daily responsibilities, replacing it with increased time for prayer. The monastery at Cluny reached the height of its power and influence in the twelfth century, overseeing more than three hundred monasteries throughout Europe.[12]

Zinzendorf and the Moravians, 1722

Count Nikolaus Ludwig von Zinzendorf was born in 1700 in Dresden, Germany. In 1722, Zinzendorf bought an estate in Berthelsdorf,

Germany, from his grandmother and offered refuge in his newly purchased estate to a group of persecuted Moravian Christians known as the Unitas Fratrum. These Moravians were the remnant following of the reformer John Huss. Since the 1600s, these saints had suffered under the hands of successive repressive Catholic monarchs.[13] On Zinzendorf's Berthelsdorf estate, they formed the community of Herrnhut, the "watch of the Lord," which quickly grew to around three hundred. Due to divisions and tension among the Moravians, Zinzendorf became the leader of the community and created a new spiritual constitution for the brethren.

On August 13, 1727, the power of God came down upon a prayer meeting in the Berthelsdorf church.[14] (This day is commonly referred to as the Moravian Pentecost.) The move of the Spirit was so profound among the members of the community that they stayed up all night, not wanting the power of God to wane. Within two weeks of the outpouring, twenty-four men and twenty-four women made a covenant to each pray for one hour every day. Leviticus 6:13 became their banner scripture: "The fire must be kept burning on the altar continuously; it must not go out" (NIV). Soon, seventy people had committed to pray continuously, and their prayer meeting grew and continued unabated for over one hundred years!

From the prayer rooms of Herrnhut, the modern Protestant missions movement was birthed. The missionary zeal that possessed the Moravians was unprecedented in church history. For instance, Protestants typically send out one missionary for every five thousand members of their denomination. The Moravians, however, had a much higher ratio, sending out 226 missionaries by the year 1776. That's one missionary for every sixty members! We will never know the full impact the Moravians had in world evangelism, but we do know that they strongly influenced William Carey, the father of modern missions,[15] as well as John Wesley.[16] The impact of this little community of persecuted believers, committed to seeking the face of God night and day, has truly been immeasurable.

In 1733, only six years after the night-and-day prayer meeting started in Herrnhut, a religious revival broke out in Northampton, Massachusetts, led by a thirty-year-old Presbyterian preacher named Jonathan Edwards. This revival was the initial spark of the First Great Awakening, which swept through the United States and Europe. Did the night-and-day prayer from Herrnhut release something in the Spirit that prepared the earth for this First Great Awakening?

When considering even this brief glimpse of church history, it's easy to see that the church has a rich heritage of night-and-day prayer. Historically, God has raised up a devoted people of prayer to prepare the world through intercession for every great move of His Spirit. As we now take a look at the contemporary prayer movement, we see this same pattern reflected, and gain a sense of what God has ordained for this hour in the earth.

Notes

1. Saint Nikolai Velemirovic, "Prologue of Ohrid: July 3," Western American Diocese: Serbian Orthodox Church in North and South America, last modified April 4, 2014, http://www.westsrbdio.org/en/prologue/558-july-3.

2. "A Brief History of 24/7 Prayer: The Early Monastic Tradition of 24/7 Prayer," International House of Prayer of Kansas City, last modified July 23, 2013, http://www.ihopkc.org/prayerroom/history.

3. Francis Mershman, s.v. "St. Maurice," The Catholic Encyclopedia, ed. Charles G. Herbermann, et al., vol. 10, (New York: Robert Appleton Company, 1913), last modified November 5, 2013, http://en.wikisource.org/wiki/Catholic_Encyclopedia_(1913)/St._Maurice.

4. "St. Maurice's Abbey," Wikipedia: The Free Encyclopedia, accessed December 4, 2014, http://en.wikipedia.org/wiki/St._Maurice%27s_Abbey.

5. "Continual Prayer," Wikipedia: The Free Encyclopedia, last modified April 7, 2014, http://en.wikipedia.org/wiki/Continual_prayer.

6. Jocelin, *The Most Ancient Lives of Saint Patrick* (Charleston, SC: BiblioBazaar, 2007) Reader e-book.

7. Edward D'Alton, "Bangor Abbey," The Catholic Encyclopedia, vol. 2, December 4, 2014, http://www.newadvent.org/cathen/02250a.htm.

8. James MacCaffrey, s. v. "St. Comgall," The Catholic Encyclopedia, vol. 2, accessed November 11, 2014, http://www.newadvent.org/cathen/04152c.htm.

9. Dan Graves, "Irish Abbot Comgall," Christianity.com, last modified May 2007, http://www.christianity.com/church/church-history/timeline/601-900/irish-abbot-comgall-11629719.html.

10. "Cluny Abbey," Wikipedia: The Free Encyclopedia, last modified July 13, 2014, http://en.wikipedia.org/wiki/Cluny_Abbey,

11. "Odo of Cluny," Wikipedia: The Free Encyclopedia, last modified September 30, 2013, http://en.wikipedia.org/wiki/Odo_of_Cluny.

12. George C. Alston, "Congregation of Cluny," The Catholic Encyclopedia, 4 vol., (New York: Robert Appleton Company, 1908), accessed December 4, 2014, http://www.newadvent.org/cathen/04073a.htm.

13. "Moravian Church," Wikipedia: The Free Encyclopedia, last modified July 21, 2014, http://en.wikipedia.org/wiki/Moravian_Church.

14. "The Origin & Growth," Unitas Fratrum: The Moravian Unity of the World Wide Moravian Church, accessed December 4, 2014, http://www.unitasfratrum.org/index.php/origin-growth-of-the-unitas-fratrum/.

15. Ibid.

16. "The Moravians and John Wesley," *Christian History & Biography* 1, Published electronically January 1, 1982, http://www.ctlibrary.com/ch/1982/issue1/128.html.

7

Night-and-Day Prayer in the Earth Today

W HEN I BEGAN RESEARCHING THE prayer movement for this book, I was already aware that God was multiplying prayer in a mighty way across the nations. But as I inventoried the vast number of ministries focusing on night-and-day prayer, I was struck by the magnitude of the movement. The viral expansion of so many substantial prayer initiatives is unprecedented in the history of the church. No continent is excluded. Many streams of Christianity are participating in this powerful phenomenon of perpetual prayer. And in recent days, partnerships between prayer ministries and large mission organizations have caused the volume of prayer to further escalate. Like the morning sun cresting the horizon, the prayer movement is just beginning to engulf the globe.

In this chapter, I want to draw your attention to several of the current expressions of night-and-day prayer as examples of this burgeoning movement. When we consider that these ministries are only a representative sample from a vast number of others engaging in night-and-day prayer, it becomes clear that the Lord has chosen this generation, like no other, to raise up a prayer movement across the nations of the earth.

As we consider the global prayer movement today, we must ask ourselves why. Why now? Why is the Lord building prayer in such an aggressive way? What does the Lord have in store for the generation in which He initiates a global torrent of intercession, as He has in our day?

With these questions in mind, let's consider one of the Lord's grand purposes for prayer, as portrayed in Revelation 5.

Bowls of Prayer

> Then He came and took the scroll out of the right hand of Him who sat on the throne. Now when He had taken the scroll, the four living creatures and the twenty-four elders fell down before the Lamb, each having a harp, and golden bowls *full of incense*, which are the prayers of the saints. (Revelation 5:7–8)

John reports a stunning truth here: the prayers of the saints not only ascend unobstructed to the throne, but also fill golden bowls as incense before God. It's an awesome thought that through all of history each prayer of every saint has not only been heard, but has remained before God as a perpetual petition. These prayers ever rise before Him, ministering to His heart and beckoning Him to act.

God has placed an immeasurable dignity upon the human race: He actually values our weak petitions. He doesn't hear our cries just to quickly dismiss them. God *delights* in the prayers of His people. He keeps them before Him forever, allowing them to continually echo before His throne.

The fact that the bowls are full *before* Jesus takes the scroll from the Father's hand demonstrates the essential place of prayer at the end of the age. The scroll can be considered as God's end-time action plan. Jesus takes the scroll from the Father and opens its seals to initiate the judgment events that culminate in His second coming. It is only *after* the bowls of prayer are full that Jesus takes the scroll and looses it seals. Think of it—when the bowls holding our prayers have reached their tipping point, the events of the end of the age depicted in the book of Revelation will unfold. The global prayer movement is the catalyst that causes God to initiate His end-time plans.

Isaiah declared that when the judgments of the Lord are unleashed upon the earth people will learn righteousness.[1] Through His perfect leadership, God will simultaneously release judgment and mercy on the earth through the instrument of our intercessions.

A day is coming when the golden bowls of prayer in heaven will be filled. Will our generation see the inception of this end-time drama? Today, with the global emergence of many night-and-day prayer ministries, it is reasonable to conclude that such a climax is closer than ever before.

Modern Prayer Ministries with a Night-and-Day Focus

Prayer Mountain, Seoul, South Korea
In 1958, David Yonggi Cho founded the Yoido Full Gospel Church with only a handful of people in attendance. The church began to grow, adding one thousand members within three years. By the early 1970s, the church had reached over ten thousand members. In 1973, the church founded Prayer Mountain, which was to serve as a secluded place for believers to seek the Lord privately in prayer and fasting. With over two hundred prayer grottoes available twenty-four hours a day, Prayer Mountain's daily ministry services and ceaseless worship and prayer began to attract thousands of visitors. It soon became an epicenter for intercession, sparking spiritual awakening throughout Seoul, Korea.

Today, over one million people annually frequent the serene prayer center. As a result of Cho's prayer initiative, his church rapidly expanded. Now, decades after the conception of Prayer Mountain, Yoido Full Gospel Church has become the world's largest official church, boasting over 830,000 members.[2]

Undoubtedly, Pastor Cho's earnest desire to see night-and-day prayer established in South Korea has paved the way for other ministries to enter the global prayer movement. It is likely that the incense rising to God from South Korea over the last few decades has helped give birth to the prayer movement that is sweeping the globe today.

International House of Prayer, Kansas City, Missouri, USA
In September 1999, a prayer meeting began in Kansas City that has yet to cease. A vision that was over fifteen years in the making became a reality at the International House of Prayer of Kansas City, led by Mike Bickle. Beginning with a "Gideon company" of intercessors who were committed to the mandate of ceaseless worship and prayer, this missional community has continued in unbroken worship-led prayer meetings to this day. Staffed by missionaries who have chosen intercession as their first activity of missions work, the prayer room now hosts tens of thousands of visitors each year.

Each week, eighty-four two-hour prayer meetings are led by worship teams and attended by hosts of hungry believers seeking the Lord with prayer and fasting. The community embraces 24/7 prayer as a lifestyle, while walking out its core values of intimacy with God, intercession for kingdom breakthrough, outreach and acts of justice, and spiritual preparation for the end times.[3]

As a result of this community's commitment to night-and-day prayer, hundreds of similar houses of prayer have sprung up around the world—throughout the United States and in many other nations, including Austria, Germany, the Czech Republic, the United Kingdom, Switzerland, Romania, Turkey, Israel, Lebanon, Egypt, Canada, Mexico, Colombia, South Africa, Uganda, Kenya, China, Taiwan, Thailand, and New Zealand.

International House of Prayer, Atlanta, Georgia, USA
The International House of Prayer–Atlanta is one such community birthed out of the missions base in Kansas City. In February 2006, Atlanta became the second American city to host ceaseless, worship-led prayer. Intercessors and worshipers have since manned the

prayer room every hour of every day at the International House of Prayer–Atlanta. The missions base in Atlanta closely resembles the IHOPKC model, with two-hour sets of live worship and intercession continuing consecutively and covering all 168 hours of the week.

24-7 Prayer International, London, UK

Started by a group of young people in Chichester, England, in 1999, the initial prayer room was sustained by individuals taking one-hour blocks of time to cover twenty-four hours a day. What began as one prayer room in southern England exploded across the globe, spreading into over one hundred countries and spawning thousands of prayer rooms that have engaged in twenty-four-hour prayer watches for weeks, and even months, at a time.

The mission of 24-7 Prayer is to transform the world through movements and communities of Christ-centered, mission-minded prayer. By returning to the simplest, most basic things of the Christian life—fasting, prayer, outreach to the lost, and ministry to the oppressed—the movement has had a dramatic impact upon the church across the globe. Through prayer coupled with multiple evangelistic and justice initiatives the goal of 24-7 is ultimately to transform society and turn the tide of youth culture. Their revolutionary approach to Christianity and culture has caused the media to take notice of the movement, featuring it in newspapers and magazines from *Rolling Stone* to *Reader's Digest*.[4]

TheCall, Pasadena, California, USA

In September 2000, through a dramatic series of events, Lou Engle rallied believers to gather on the Mall in Washington, DC, for a day of fasting and prayer for revival in America. Though TheCall did not publish lists of speakers or publicize big-name bands, an estimated four hundred thousand believers convened that day in a solemn assembly to pray for mercy on America.[5]

Since then, TheCall has hosted multiple gatherings in America and abroad that draw hundreds of thousands annually for a day of concentrated fasting and prayer. For example, on July 7, 2007 (07/07/07), over seventy thousand people gathered in Nashville, Tennessee, to fast and pray that God would shift the tide of sexual permissiveness that has so gripped America over the last forty years. Each event is described as a solemn assembly, patterned after the biblical mandate found in the book of Joel: "'Now, therefore,' says the LORD, 'Turn to Me with all your heart, with fasting, with weeping, and with mourning . . . gather the people, sanctify the congregation, assemble the elders . . .'" (Joel 2:12, 16).

TheCall continues to facilitate large prayer events and extended fasts worldwide. Hundreds of thousands have been mobilized in prayer and fasting through TheCall's events and various initiatives.

Global Day of Prayer, Cape Town, South Africa

The Global Day of Prayer is an annual event that organizes Christians worldwide to unite in a day of prayer and repentance. In July 2000, the Lord gave a South African businessman, Graham Power, a vision to see South Africa unite in a day of repentance and prayer. In 2002, the vision expanded to encompass all of Africa, and 2004 saw the invitation extend to the world.

Since its initial meeting in 2001, the Global Day of Prayer has seen millions of Christians from 220 nations gather on the same day for a concert of prayer that spans the globe. Stadiums around the earth are filled with repentant believers petitioning heaven to heal their nations. Through superb administration and execution, the organization has been able to touch the far reaches of the globe and fuse together believers from all denominations across nearly every nation.[6]

Although the Global Day of Prayer only lasts for one day each year, its significance should not be underestimated. Through globalization, the Global Day of Prayer team has accomplished something unprecedented in organizing a worldwide chorus of prayer and worship to Jesus. And, looking past the day of prayer itself, their team has mobilized millions into lifestyles of prayer.

Burn 24-7, Harrisburg, Pennsylvania, USA

Burn 24-7 is a traveling ministry seeking to plant sustainable prayer operations throughout the earth. Through its ministry hubs in the United States, United Kingdom, and South Africa it equips ministry bases in over two hundred international cities. Its emphasis on the core practices of Christianity—worship, prayer, and evangelism—paves the way for the communities it visits to be transformed by the power of God. Burn 24-7 is rooted in night-and-day prayer with a specific emphasis on short- and long-term missions as well as community development.

Upon arrival in a city, the ministry organizes multiple groups to come together at a "burn," which is a twenty-four-hour or longer non-stop worship and prayer meeting, divided into two-hour sessions. The goal is to see these gatherings cause a spiritual shift in the regions in which they are held.

Burn 24-7's mobile planting focus provides the prayer movement with a necessary vehicle for the worldwide establishment of night-and-day prayer. The ministry desires to see praise given to the Lord from every corner of the earth.[7]

Justice Houses of Prayer

Washington, DC, Boston, New York City, San Diego, and San Francisco all host Justice Houses of Prayer. These JHOP communities operate on extensive prayer schedules, having a specific intercessory focus on modern issues of justice, from abortion to human trafficking. This ministry is closely associated with TheCall, praying daily for the specific initiatives TheCall targets in their larger corporate gatherings.

Succat Hallel, Jerusalem, Israel

Since 2004, hundreds of intercessors have taken their place in a Jerusalem-based prayer house that overlooks Mount Zion. They are contending night and day until the Lord makes Jerusalem a praise in the earth (Isa. 62:7). The house of prayer is named Succat Hallel, which is Hebrew for "tabernacle of praise." The Succat Hallel community hosts intercessors from over five continents and offers short-term internships for those who desire to pray on-site for the city of Jerusalem.

Isaiah 62 records God's declaration to set up intercessors who will pray around the clock for Jerusalem and never hold their peace. These intercessors are likened to watchmen, who take their place on the wall of prayer, crying out for Jerusalem until the city shines in righteousness.

Youth With A Mission (YWAM) University of the Nations, Kona, Hawaii

Youth With A Mission is one of the largest missions organizations in the earth, with over eighteen thousand full-time missionaries working in over 180 nations on the earth. The largest base is found in Kona, Hawaii. At the center of this powerful missions organization is a house of prayer that operates a weekly schedule of forty hours of prayer and worship. In addition, each month the prayer room runs a live twenty-four-hour worship and prayer meeting. The prayer room in Kona is being replicated in YWAM bases throughout the world.[8]

Various Cities

Prayer ministries geared toward a sustainable expression of night-and-day prayer are beginning to surface in several cities across the earth. Hong Kong, for example, has four different prayer ministries that endeavor to fulfill a 24/7 prayer schedule. London hosts a house of prayer operating on a significant prayer schedule, ultimately desiring to run perpetually. Amsterdam, Bogotá, Cairo, Chicago, Jakarta, Jerusalem, Pretoria, Tauranga, and many other cities around the world host at least one 24/7-minded prayer ministry.

Night-and-Day Prayer: More Than a Ministry Trend

Without question, night-and-day prayer is rapidly expanding to cities across the globe. Participation in these ministries is increasing, allowing for greater sustainability, and enabling prayer to penetrate every region of the earth.

As we take note of this pattern, let's consider Jesus' question in Luke 18:8: "When the Son of Man comes, will He really find faith on the earth?" Jesus was essentially asking, "Who will be faithful to cry out night and day in prayer (vv. 1, 7) in the generation in which I return?"

If we consider all of this together, we can see that God is raising up night-and-day prayer across the earth for more than simply starting an exciting ministry trend. These prayer ministries serve a significant purpose. I believe night-and-day prayer *will* be preserved until Jesus comes, that He might find a faithful praying bride on the earth in the generation in which He returns. Let our hearts be encouraged by the rapid escalation of continual prayer, and let us consider the profundity of this movement, for it has been divinely ordained and initiated in this hour.

In light of this proliferation of night-and-day prayer, we must ask the Lord what our part in it is. I encourage you to question Him as to how He desires you, individually, to participate. It is evident that He is establishing night-and-day prayer across the nations. The question becomes, how shall we respond?

Notes

1. Isaiah 26:9.

2. "Yoido Full Gospel Church," Wikipedia: The Free Encyclopedia, last modified: June 6, 2014, http://en.wikipedia.org/wiki/Yoido_Full_Gospel_Church.

3. "About the International House of Prayer," International House of Prayer of Kansas City, last modified July 28, 2011, http://www.ihopkc.org/about/.

4. "What Is 24-7 Prayer?" 24-7 Prayer: Prayer, Mission and Justice, accessed November 11, 2014, http://www.24-7prayer.com/about/what.

5. "Our History," TheCall, accessed November 11, 2014, http://thecall.com/Publisher/Article.aspx?ID=1000104029.

6. "History," The Global Day of Prayer, accessed November 11, 2014, http://www.globaldayofprayer.com/history.html.

7. "What is Burn 24-7," Burn 24-7, accessed December 4, 2014, http://www.burn24-7.com/about#.VIDKvpPF_R0.

8. "About Us," YWAM Youth With A Mission Worldwide, accessed November 12, 2014, www.ywam.org/about-us/.

The Single Most Compelling Reason

W E'VE SPENT THE PREVIOUS CHAPTERS establishing the biblical and historic precedents for night-and-day prayer. However compelling this evidence might be in proving the validity of night-and-day prayer, it is not the most compelling reason for its practice.

One concept stands alone as the essential rationale for sustaining continuous worship and prayer before the Lord. But before I mention it I want to ask you to step back and consider Jesus.

What is Jesus worth to you? How can His worth be measured? Shall we put a monetary figure on Him? Horrifyingly, that has already been done. His betrayer thought that the thirty pieces of silver it took to buy a slave was sufficient. Judas' folly was not simply in valuing the eternal One as a slave; the folly was in valuing Him by any natural measure at all.

How can we attribute a price to Him who is matchless, without comparison, without equal, the very definition of beauty and rarity? Nothing created can possibly compare to the worth of Him who is *uncreated*.

The wonder of this mystery is towering: the uncreated God wrapped Himself in human flesh. God came to us in a frail human frame. Nothing could be a greater shock or scandal. His greatness, shrouded in human finiteness, is incomprehensible to our sensibilities. How could the perfect One put on humanity? How could the flawless One come to dwell in a flawed and fallen world?

Breathe it in for a moment—He who is all rare, all fair, all beautiful, all majestic, all perfect came under the yoke of mortality. And His humility doesn't end there. In finality, He who is life succumbed to death's authority. Gasp, and consider the unthinkable reality of God in the flesh, and then gasp again at the impossible truth of His death at human hands. Though a familiar thought, it's one that should never cease to cause us to tremble—God became a man and died for man by the hands of man.

And why? What could be the reason for this inestimable humiliation?

Love.

His is a love that compels deity to denigrate itself by dwelling amidst fallen humanity. His is a love that humiliates itself by succumbing to the demonic desire of His own torture. His is a love that gives excessively to the point of feeling shame on behalf of its recipients. It's an awkward love that apparently far outweighs the value of the beloved. Yet it's a love all true, all pure, all secure.

Jesus' journey into humanity was for the singular purpose of redeeming men for God[1] in order that He might express His love and mercy toward us eternally.[2]

When taken all together—His eminence, His extravagant love, and the exorbitant price He paid for us—it is nearly unmanageable. We almost cannot bear to glimpse this Man of love, with His overwhelming offering that was seemingly completely out of step with reality.

Shall we really believe that we are worth His life? Shall we actually agree that His death was a rightly valued payment for us? Pause and digest this truth—*we are worth it to Him.*

You are worth His life and death. It was because of His own desire that He measured the trade, His life for yours, and esteemed you worth it. He wanted intimacy with you so much that He willingly and joyfully traded Himself for you.

Those who wrestle with these truths tend to respond in one of two ways: turn away in disbelief, or be overcome by their weightiness. Those of us who have submitted to Jesus have surely experienced the latter. Jesus' sacrifice for us overcomes our stubbornness and ultimately defeats all our objections.

How Shall We Respond?

Once we are won to His love, the question remains: what response is reasonable to offer in return for the lavish gift we have received? It's not that we have to pay off our debt. That would be impossible. It's that we long to answer His sacrificial love with a loving expenditure of our own.

So what *is* Jesus worth?

Is He worth your time? Your attention? Your energy? Your love?

How much? How much is He worth to you?

Before you answer, I want to remind you how much you are worth to Him. Pause now, again, and consider His humility and sacrifice.

A true glimpse of Jesus' worth calls our souls to respond. When we see Him, even a little, a hard-wired response bubbles up from deep within our hearts to give all that we are in abandonment to Him.

To love the Lord God with all our heart, mind, soul, and strength is the natural response of the soul that has understood and encountered the depths of His love.

Which now brings us to the most compelling reason for night-and-day prayer: Jesus is worthy of it.

He is worthy of worship every second of every minute of every hour of every day. When I'm asked why we do night-and-day prayer, the answer is simple: Jesus is worthy of it. When the question comes, "How can you worship Him twenty-four hours a day?" the simple answer is, "How can we *not* worship Him twenty-four hours a day?"

Jesus is worthy of all of our love, all of our time, and all of our attention. He is the pearl of great price, for whom, when we find Him, we sell all that we have, out of joy, in order to "buy" Him.

The anthem rings through the throne room of heaven: "Worthy is the Lamb who was slain to receive power and riches and wisdom, and strength and honor and glory and blessing."[3] Since He is worthy to receive from us all that we have and all that we are, He must be worthy of worship all day and all night.

Greater than all the other evidence, the matchless worth of the Son of God is the answer that trumps all objections to night-and-day prayer.

Jesus is truly worthy.

Notes

1. Revelation 5:9.
2. Ephesians 2:4, 7.
3. Revelation 5:12.

9

Speedy Justice

Then He spoke a parable to them, that men always ought to pray and not lose heart, saying, "There was in a certain city a judge who did not fear God nor regard man. Now there was a widow in that city; and she came to him, saying, 'Get justice for me from my adversary.' And he would not for a while; but afterward he said within himself, 'Though I do not fear God nor regard man, yet because this widow troubles me I will avenge her, lest by her continual coming she weary me.'" Then the Lord said, "Hear what the unjust judge said. And shall God not avenge His own elect who cry out day and night to Him, though He bears long with them? I tell you that He will avenge them speedily. Nevertheless, when the Son of Man comes, will He really find faith on the earth?"

LUKE 18:1–8

THROUGHOUT THE SCRIPTURES, CERTAIN PASSAGES function as beacons of light, greatly illuminating our path. They provide foundational understanding of the topics they discuss. The parable of the unjust judge is one such passage, offering us a cornerstone of revelation regarding prayer. Too often, biblical topics like prayer are understood through our human lenses, lacking the proper biblical plumb line to anchor us to truth. This parable functions as an anchor for us regarding God's perspective on prayer and how ceaseless prayer is integral to God's plan at the end of the age. In this chapter, we will consider this parable and its application, which are essential to the end-time prayer movement.

The Purpose of the Parable

Jesus uses this parable to describe the condition of the earth during the season of His return.[1] In chapter 18, Jesus then tells the parable of the unjust judge, concluding by again referencing the time of His second coming (Luke 18:8). Though the parable is applicable to believers of every generation, it would be a mistake to ignore its obvious context. Therefore, we should primarily consider this parable as an admonition to believers on the earth just prior to the time of the Lord's return.

Many parables do not explicitly state their purpose, but here Luke tells us the twofold reason that Jesus spoke this parable: to motivate men to pray without ceasing and to keep them from giving up.

In the past, when I read through this text, I actually felt *discouraged* from prayer rather than *encouraged*. I knew I must be missing something, but I could not put my finger on it. I had misunderstood Jesus' purpose in telling the parable, and therefore misinterpreted His words. I realized that since I was actually discouraged instead of encouraged in prayer, I needed to reread it, asking the Lord for revelation until I experienced the courage the parable promised to bring. Once the light went on, this parable became a great source of help to me in my journey of prayer.

The parable of the unjust judge, briefly paraphrased, is this. A certain individual had illegally defrauded a widow, who filed her complaint with the local judge, hoping for justice to be served. Instead, the judge did nothing. He was a godless man, unconcerned with the widow's plight. She repeatedly brought her case before him until finally, because of her persistence, he arrested the guilty one. Ultimately, the judge was not moved by compassion; he was moved by the widow's unyielding resolve and continuous requests.

Contrast, Not Comparison

At a glance, it may seem that the unjust judge represents the eternal Father and that the widow is a picture of believers. However, Jesus is not giving us a straightforward comparison; instead, He is contrasting the figures. Here is where the truth of this parable came alive for me: God is not like the unjust judge; instead, He is the exact opposite. He is the God of perfect justice, the avenger of all who are defrauded.[2] He's not unjust in any of His ways.

Similarly, the widow is not a picture of the bride, but rather the antithesis. The church is forever joined to Jesus, never to be widowed. The widow has no relationship or influence with the judge, whereas the church's position with Jesus is fully established. We are seated with Him in heavenly places and are the very object of His favor and affection.

In literature, this type of comparison is known as an "a fortiori" argument, in which the first example is given to illustrate the clear truth of the second. Jesus encourages us by saying, "Do you hear what the unjust judge said?" In other words, if a godless, unjust judge will actually execute justice on behalf a widow, how much more will God, who is enthroned on justice, vindicate His beloved ones who pray to Him night and day?

In contrast to the unjust judge, Jesus rhetorically asks, "Will not God bring about justice for His chosen ones . . . Will he keep putting them off?" The answer is clear—God will *not* put off His people who cry out to Him day and night. He *will* answer them speedily!

Let these truths sink deep down into your soul. God is not unjust, and you are not a spiritual widow. Though it may seem that you continue to cry out over the same issues with no discernible change, God hears your cry and is answering your prayer.

Jesus finishes the parable by asking an important question, "In the day that I return, will I find faith on the earth?" He is not questioning whether there will be people of faith alive at the time of His coming. Instead, He is *instructing* us with this question, specifically addressing the concepts introduced in the parable. He is actually saying, "I want My people to be relentlessly contending in prayer *night and day* at the time of My return to the earth. Who will engage with My plan and not give up?"

The Fainting Spirit

One of the great challenges intercessors face is discouragement. Those who have prayed long hours know the pain of adjuring heaven, only to be met with delays and seemingly unanswered prayer. At times, burdens of intercession are incredibly weighty and urgent. When we don't immediately see answers, we are tempted to discount the effectiveness of our prayers. We judge our success by discernible results rather than by God's delight in our obedience.

At other times, as intercessors, our constant engagement in spiritual conflict causes weariness in our souls. We pray earnestly, neglecting to take care of our physical, emotional, and spiritual needs. Ultimately, we find ourselves exhausted and we lose faith in prayer. Both discouragement and fatigue are reasons we give up before we see the fruit of our intercession. Many times I have found myself spiritually worn out through intense seasons of intercession. When the answers were delayed, my heart began to teeter-totter into doubt. The truths in this parable are meant for those moments.

Jesus told the parable to give us a vision for perseverance. He wants us to press on in prayer and not lose heart, no matter the delay or the challenges we face. Jesus assures us that the Father will not move one moment too late. He will answer our cries, and *speedily*. He admonishes us to persistently hammer away in intercession until we see breakthrough, rather than becoming discouraged by what seems to be a delayed response from God. The Father longs to execute justice for His people. The point is, when we cry out continually, we will see the answers to our prayers as we persevere by God's grace.

Understanding Justice

Jesus promised that those who call upon Him *will* receive justice. But what does "justice" mean? What is He is actually promising?

Biblically, justice is God working on behalf of the orphan, the widow, the foreigner, the poor, and the oppressed.[3] Another simple definition is "God making all the wrong things right."

Injustices have harmed many people in many generations throughout the earth. Issues such as human trafficking, abortion, poverty, racism, and fatherlessness plague societies in every sphere of the globe. Additionally, there are grievous spiritual injustices, including sickness, disease, and demonic oppression. Ultimately, justice is *liberty to all who are captive*. God longs to be gracious to us, to rid the earth of its injustices, and to bring healing and salvation to all who are oppressed.

Night-and-Day as the Prerequisite

In the parable, Jesus tells us that the necessary requirement for seeing justice released is His people seeking Him *night and day*. Many desire to see God move in great acts of justice, but they overlook this prescribed requisite of night-and-day prayer.

In the generation of the Lord's return there will be more injustices in the earth than ever before.[4] God's antidote to this wickedness is night-and-day prayer. As His people engage His heart, bringing before Him their cries for His intervention, He will answer with power. The final act of justice is the return of the Lord Jesus.

Isaiah proclaimed that Jesus will return with vengeance in His heart to bring justice to every sphere of every society on earth.[5] He will come as a mighty man of war to vindicate all the oppressed.[6] He knows intimately the plight of every person who has ever been victimized. He will not let one injustice remain unanswered. He will make all the wrong things right, heal every wounded heart, and vindicate all who have been abused. When He comes, He will see to it that justice prevails throughout the earth.[7]

This is the reason He called us to pray night and day. He spoke this parable to encourage us to contend without quitting until justice is wrought throughout the earth. He has given us the necessary ingredients to see massive breakthroughs that will culminate in His second coming. If this is His promise, how shall we not hurl ourselves into the fray, praying night and day until justice is established? Let us partner with His heart until we see every vestige of corruption expelled. Let's give ourselves to prayer night and day until righteousness reigns and justice rolls like a mighty river.[8]

Notes

1. Luke 17:22–37.
2. 1 Thessalonians 4:6.
3. Psalm 146:7–9.
4. Daniel 8:23; 2 Timothy 3:1–5.
5. Isaiah 42:2–4.
6. Isaiah 42:13.
7. Isaiah 11:4–5; 16:5; cf. Psalm 72:2–4; 98:9.
8. Amos 5:24.

10

God's Plan for Israel's Salvation

For Zion's sake I will not hold My peace, and for Jerusalem's sake I will not rest, until her righteousness goes forth as brightness, and her salvation as a lamp that burns.

ISAIAH 62:1

God's HEART FOR JUSTICE IS one of the primary reasons He is raising up a global prayer movement. Another issue also burns deeply in the heart of the eternal Father, one that many of us in the church do not fully understand. It is so important, that He will not hold His peace, nor rest until His desire regarding this issue is accomplished. He will not relent until this yearning of His heart is fulfilled. What is the cause of such deep passion in the heart of God? For many, the answer is a side issue, something that seems ancillary to the "main and plain" of Christianity. However, this issue is not at all ancillary to God. It is of utmost importance, and central to the story line of His dealings with all humanity. What is it that causes His heart to burn with such zeal? What is it that is so important to Him that He will not rest until it is accomplished? The salvation of 100 percent of the people of the nation of Israel.

For many years I didn't understand what the Scriptures clearly conveyed regarding God's plan for Israel. I had heard that Israel was important to Christianity, and that we, as Christians, needed to pray for the peace of Jerusalem. Yet I had no real understanding

of the importance of Israel to the entire story line of the Bible, nor
to the heart of the Lord. Only within the last several years have I
begun to comprehend God's zeal over this people, who seem to be
continually at the center of international controversy.

To truly know God's heart, we must understand what is in
the Scriptures regarding the nation of Israel. By the inspiration of
the Holy Spirit, Paul declared that all Israel would be saved.[1] Paul
wanted to inform the Roman believers of God's plan to save the
remnant of Israel at the end of the age. All believers must comprehend that God has a plan for His chosen people, Israel. I personally
believe that this verse refers to the salvation of every Jew who will
be alive on the planet at the time of Jesus' return. Never before
has the earth seen a nation one hundred percent born again. Yet,
in the generation in which the Lord returns, all of Israel shall be
saved. This truth is burning in the Lord's heart, and He wants our
hearts to burn with His—so that we love the people He loves and
pray for their salvation.

Sovereign Election

Psalm 113:6 declares that our God humbles Himself when He
beholds things in heaven and earth. Consider the greatness of our
God: He is so superior to all of His creation that it is incredibly
humbling for Him to even *look* upon His creation. He is highly
exalted over all His works. He is the sovereign God of the entire
universe. All things came into being and are held together by His
very word.

His ways and thoughts are far superior to ours. In this age,
we are only able to understand a small fragment of His plans. Yet,
at the same time, the things that we *are* able to comprehend are
enough to thrill us all the days of our lives.

God's eternal purposes are beyond our comprehension. He
continually makes decisions according to His sovereign plans, and
the reasoning behind His plans are not immediately apparent to
us, because we lack the information that only He possesses. He

knows *everything* and accomplishes *everything* that He desires in perfection, according to His eternal purposes. His ways and decisions are infinitely higher than our own.

In this age, even the most spiritually sensitive, prophetic person only sees "in a mirror dimly" (1 Corinthians 13:12). It is God's choice and privilege to reveal to us or to veil from us whatever He desires.

Undoubtedly, God's election and choice of Israel is veiled to even the most insightful among us. When considering God's choice of Israel we must agree that His manifold purposes are at times beyond what we can fully comprehend in this age. He is the sovereign God, who operates all things flawlessly. Since He is perfect and all that He does is perfect, we can ascertain that His choice of Israel is perfect.

It's important for us to understand that God has chosen Israel for Himself, according to His own purposes. Though only eternity will fully reveal to us all the reasoning behind His choice, we can derive from Scripture some of the details behind His reasoning. Let's take a look at some of the reasons Scripture gives here.

A Special Treasure

In God's address to Israel at the onset of the exodus from Egypt, we find the first of several reasons for His choice.

> "Now therefore, if you will indeed obey My voice and keep My covenant, then you shall be a special treasure to Me above all people." (Exodus 19:5)

God chose the people of Israel to be a "special treasure" to Him. The New International Version translates the phrase as "treasured possession." At times we overlook the fact that God yearns for intimacy with people. His heart burns with passion to give and to receive love. He Himself *is* love, and therefore He *must* love. Love that does not give is not love at all. God wanted to selflessly give love to those who had the option of rejecting His love. God has always desired intimacy with all the people of His creation.

When He carried Israel out of Egypt so that they might worship Him in the desert, we see the very core of God's desire for all the nations. He chose Israel to be a people who would voluntarily love Him, with whom He could express the affections of His heart as a template for relationship with the rest of the nations.

God's foremost motive for everything that He does is love. Therefore, when He chose the nation of Israel, He chose them because of love. They were the undeserving recipients of His heavenly affections. Though they have almost totally rejected their Messiah, when He returns they will turn from their hardness of heart, and, with weeping and repentance, embrace Him as their King and God.[2] They will be the example to all the earth of what it means to live as God's special treasure.

A Kingdom of Priests

In the next verse we find a second reason for God's choice.

"You will be for me a kingdom of priests and a holy nation." (Exodus 19:6, NIV)

God wanted Israel to be a nation who embodied the ministry of priesthood unto Him. Because God longs for intimacy, He wanted to give His people access to His heart and His emotions; He desires to give and receive love from men. Just as priests are called to stand before God and bless Him with worship and adoration, Israel was to serve the Lord as a kingdom of priests—as a nation who would not only minister to God's heart, but would also minister *on behalf* of God to the hearts of men.

God raised up Israel as an example of what He would do for the nation whose people would fully give themselves to Him. He declared to Israel that He would bless them abundantly if they would serve and obey Him.[3] By separating this people unto Himself and blessing them greatly, He would provoke all nations of the earth to seek this same intimacy with their Creator.

Never has the earth seen an entire nation whose people have given themselves completely in abandonment to God. However, in the coming age, all Israel will be possessed with the "spirit of burning," completely filled with passion and desire for the Lord.[4] They will serve the Lord with fervent zeal. In that day, the nations of the earth will be drawn to them because the glory of the Lord will rest upon them.[5] Isaiah tells us that in that day, many will be drawn to the Lord and converted because of Israel's righteous testimony.[6]

A Lineage for Messiah

A third reason for God's choice of Israel is understood through considering God's plan of redemption. When Adam fell into sin through Satan's lure, he forfeited intimacy with God on behalf of all mankind. But God immediately initiated an action plan to redeem the entire human race. God declared that a man would be born who would restore intimacy with God for all mankind and overcome Satan by crushing his head.[7] That man is Jesus—the Jewish carpenter from Nazareth—the Messiah. The Bible declares that Jesus disarmed every demonic force and triumphed over the enemy through the victory of the cross.[8]

Since a man forfeited intimacy with God, it was necessary for God to use another man to restore that intimacy. This man had to be born of a woman. In other words, he had to actually be human. In order for him to have the power to redeem mankind, he had to have the ability to choose either righteousness or wickedness and to meet the requirement of living a sinless life. Jesus met that requirement, and now, through His blood, we have free access to the throne of God.[9] But Jesus has not only restored us to intimacy with the eternal Father; He has also destroyed the works of the enemy in our lives.

While we may understand that Jesus is God, we sometimes forget that He is also a man. He did not just momentarily become a man and then return to being God after His resurrection. When He became a man, He became a man for eternity. He is fully God and fully man—forever. He sits, as a man, at the right hand of the Father to intercede for the rest of humanity. He is the perfect representative of God to man and of man to God. While He lived on the earth, He experienced all the challenges and temptations that we go through, yet was without sin. And so He is able to sympathize with all of our weaknesses.[10]

Since God determined to send His Son to the earth as a man, He had to choose a people through whom His Son would be born. In His sovereignty, God chose Abraham and formed the nation of Israel through his lineage. One of the divine purposes of this nation was to birth Messiah. How amazing to think that when God chose Abraham, He chose him so that He could bring forth Jesus. No wonder He is zealous for Israel with such great zeal![11]

God's Passion for Israel

The Gentiles shall see your righteousness, and all kings your glory. You shall be called by a new name, which the mouth of the LORD will name. You shall also be a crown of glory in the hand of the LORD, and a royal diadem in the hand of your God. (Isaiah 62:2–3)

Isaiah 62 is an extremely important chapter regarding God's end-time plan for Israel and how He will use night-and-day prayer to bring about her salvation. Perhaps no other verses in the Bible so clearly describe God's desire for Israel. Here, God specifically enumerates His strategy to make Zion "a praise in the earth" (Isaiah 62:7).

God is zealous to see Israel burning with salvation. He is committed to seeing the people of Israel become a "crown of glory in the hand of the Lord" (Isaiah 62:3). God is the perfection of beauty; He "wraps Himself in light as with a garment" (Psalm 104:2,

NIV). What kind of crown could possibly adorn the One who is the definition of beauty? Isaiah explains that Israel will burn with righteousness to such an extent that they will be beautiful not only to the Lord, but also to the nations of the earth. Furthermore, He declares that they shall be sought after and married to the Lord.

> You shall no longer be termed Forsaken, nor shall your land any more be termed Desolate; but you shall be called Hephzibah, and your land Beulah; for the LORD delights in you, and your land shall be married. (Isaiah 62:4)

The Lord is going to give the people of Israel a new name. Rather than being called "forsaken," they shall be called "Hephzibah," literally, "the one in whom the Lord delights." God has always delighted in His people. Though they rejected their Messiah at His first coming, God has continued to call them *His* people.[12] When He gives them their new name, all the earth will know that this is the nation in which God delights.

Before Jesus returns, the Antichrist's armies will devastate Israel, and the nations of the earth will consider her forsaken by the Lord.[13] Yet God will not leave Israel in that state. Rather than being considered desolate, they shall be called "Beulah," literally, "married." God will heal Israel's land, and all the nations of the earth will know Israel as the people who are married to the Lord. A dramatic turnaround is in store for this nation! Finally, through Isaiah the prophet, the Lord expresses His incredible delight in the nation of Israel.

> For as a young man marries a virgin, so shall your sons marry you; and as the bridegroom rejoices over the bride, so shall your God rejoice over you. (Isaiah 62:5)

God will rejoice over Israel in the same way that a newly married bridegroom rejoices over and delights in his bride. God does not call Israel to salvation simply to fulfill a contractual obligation; He is deeply in love with His people, passionately longing for them. When they come to the knowledge of Jesus as Messiah, they will experience the full measure of God's great passion and joy over them. In that day, His eternal desire for them will be fulfilled. They will give Him their love with abandoned zeal. This is a non-negotiable plan in the Lord's heart. He is burning with desire to see Israel fully in love with His Son; He is committed to and focused on the salvation of this nation.

Today, many of the people of Israel are socially "Jewish" but religiously agnostic. However, one day every nation will regard Israel as the picture of righteousness, burning with passion for her Messiah. In that day all the nations of the earth will be instructed by Israel's example. In Isaiah 60:3, the Lord declares that all nations of the earth will be drawn to Israel because of her light and beauty. God's plan for her redemption is firmly established, and He will not rest until it comes to pass. Since God's desire is so fully established in regard to this nation, we must ask ourselves what part we play in His plan.

Notes

1. Romans 11:25–26.
2. Zechariah 12:10.
3. Deuteronomy 28.
4. Isaiah 4:4.
5. Isaiah 60:1–5.
6. Hosea 2:23; Zechariah 8:23.
7. Genesis 3:15, NIV.
8. Colossians 2:15.
9. Hebrews 4:15; 7:26–27.
10. Hebrews 4:15.
11. Zechariah 8:2.
12. Romans 11:2.
13. Joel 3:2, 12; Zephaniah 3:8; Zechariah 12:2–3; 14:2; Revelation 16:14.

| 11 |

Set Watchmen

I have set watchmen on your walls, O Jerusalem; they shall never hold their peace day or night. You who make mention of the LORD, do not keep silent, and give Him no rest till He establishes and till He makes Jerusalem a praise in the earth.

ISAIAH 62:6–7

AS WE DISCUSSED IN THE previous chapter, the first five verses of Isaiah 62 clearly identify God's fervent desire to see all Israel saved. He is burning for her salvation and He will not relent. Verses 6 and 7 contain God's plan to see this desire come to pass.

Set Watchmen

The Lord declares that He has set "watchmen" on the walls of Jerusalem, who will never hold their peace day or night. These watchmen are at the center of God's strategy to bring about the full salvation of Israel.

Historically, watchmen were set upon city walls or nearby hills to look out for impending danger. They worked alongside gatekeepers, who were stationed as operators of the city gates. Watchmen had to have keen vision so that they could identify an approaching envoy. They could tell, even from far away, if those approaching were friend or foe. Once the watchmen identified who was approaching, they would instruct the gatekeepers to either open or lock the gates. If they sensed a threat to the city, the watchmen would send a warning to the king or the head of the military so that the army could prepare for the impending danger.

In these verses, the Lord uses watchmen and walls as symbols. Watchmen represent intercessors. Just as watchmen gazed into the distance to identify all who approached the city, God's people pray and receive insight regarding His plans. Similarly, when Isaiah declares that God has set watchmen "upon the walls of Jerusalem," the phrase "upon the walls" is not to be understood as an actual location; rather, it conveys the focus of God's attention—Israel. The watchmen are commissioned by God to pray that His desire concerning Israel comes to pass.

Historically, watchmen operated in battalions that worked in shifts, covering the city from sunrise to sunset and all through the night. Similarly, the Lord prophesied through Isaiah that He would raise up watchmen, plural—communities in which intercessors would engage in prayer night and day. These communities will never cease praying until salvation comes to all of Israel.

The next part of these verses identifies the watchmen as ones "who make mention of the Lord." The New International Version translates this phrase as ones "who call out to the Lord." There is no question that these watchmen are intercessors who continually cry out to the Lord in prayer.

One of the most powerful aspects of Isaiah 62:6 is that it is written in the past tense. God says, "I *have set* watchmen on your walls." Our God is the God who sees the end from the beginning. The night-and-day prayer movement in the earth is only beginning, but it will become much greater in scope and power in the coming decades. Before the end of this age, communities all over the globe will cry out to the Lord in night-and-day prayer for the salvation of Israel. *This is an already established reality in God's heart that will surely come to pass!*

Who Are These Watchmen?

How does one know if he or she is called to be "set" as a watchman? Most who feel specifically drawn to prayer or worship don't think of themselves as watchmen for Jerusalem's salvation. All they really know is that they desire to spend long hours with the Lord.

Years ago, as a youth pastor gripped with a passion for revival, I had no idea of God's plan for Israel. All I knew was that I had an insatiable hunger for God to move in power in my life —and the way to see that happen was through prayer. For years the Lord had prophetically spoken to me about being a watchman and a gatekeeper, but I had no idea what those words meant. The name of our youth ministry, "212," even spoke of the number of gatekeepers in the tabernacle of David.[1] But even though I was familiar with that verse, I did not realize what the Lord was speaking to me.

Only *after* God dealt with me about transitioning from youth ministry into planting a house of prayer did I realize He had called me to be an Isaiah-62 watchman. In reality, He had been preparing me for this mandate my entire Christian life. When that realization touched my heart, I understood what God had been saying all along. He had called me to be a watchman, an intercessor, to pray for His plans to come to pass in the earth, including Israel's salvation. Once I understood this, I was "set."

Though the entire Bible is anointed and divinely powerful, it is common for us to choose certain passages that "speak" to us as our favorites. However, there is a vast difference between a passage that speaks *to* you and a passage that speaks *about* you. I was exhilarated the first time I realized that those who are a part of the current night-and-day prayer movement are actually a living fulfillment of God's prophetic promise in Isaiah 62. Could it be that God was speaking of the modern-day prayer movement over 2,700 years ago when Isaiah prophesied these words? I believe the answer is absolutely, yes!

Never before in history has God commissioned a global company of believers to devote their lives to night-and-day prayer. The number of people who feel led to serve the Lord in this fashion is rapidly growing. I believe Isaiah 62 is specifically written about those who, in this hour, are heeding the call to cry out day and night until Zion is made a praise in the earth. As you consider these truths, I want to ask you a question: do you sense the Lord's leading upon your heart to engage with night-and-day prayer as a normal part of your Christian lifestyle? If there is even a nudge in your heart to spend long hours before the Lord in worship and prayer, I want you to consider this next question. Could it be that you are part of this watchmen company of whom Isaiah prophesied?

Though many look for supernatural signs from heaven to confirm God's leading in their lives, and at times He accommodates with such, more often God's calling does not manifest via a supernatural visitation. Most often He leads us by the inner witness of the Holy Spirit.[2] So how do you know if God is setting you as a watchman? Perhaps you feel led by the Lord to take a season of your life to serve God with prayer and fasting as your main focus. Is it possible that the reason you feel led in this direction is because God is raising up a global prayer movement all across the nations of the earth? Could it be that He had you in mind when He spoke through Isaiah of the watchmen who would pray night and day?

God sets a person as a watchman when that person *realizes* it is God's calling on his life drawing him to prayer. When this truth is revealed to the heart, it is a work of God's grace. Divine revelation upon our hearts is the primary way that God leads us into any calling. And it is the principal way in which He sets watchmen.

People cannot manufacture the desire to spend their lives in intercession and worship. On the contrary, the Scripture tells us there is "none who seeks God" (Romans 3:11). Anyone who has this desire burning in him is a living emblem of the grace of God working on the human heart. The likely reason you want to give yourself to night-and-day prayer is because God is wooing you to partner with His end-time agenda. He's been speaking about you since the days of Isaiah!

They Will Never Hold Their Peace

God says in Isaiah 62:1 that He will neither rest nor hold His peace until Israel burns with His very righteousness. In the same way, those who are set as watchmen will not rest or hold *their* peace until Zion becomes a praise in the earth. God is releasing His zeal to His end-time church so that she will cry out in intercession, empowered by His very passions for Israel. How else could broken, frail humans accomplish the massive feat of ceaselessly praying and partnering with God for the fulfillment of His divine purposes? In His grace and by His zeal, the end-time church will cry out night and day. We will never hold our peace!

The global prayer movement will not only operate in God's passion, but also in a way that mirrors worship in the heavenly throne room: night and day, on earth just as it is in heaven. God does not rest; therefore, He is raising up a people who will not rest in pursuing His purposes. They will be a people moved with His passions, in full cooperation with His plans.

Jerusalem, a Praise in the Earth

Though the prayer movement is still in its infancy compared to what it will be, the fact that it is emerging across the nations is a prophetic indicator that we are living in the season of Isaiah 62's fulfillment. Let this truth cause your heart to tremble. Who but God alone could mastermind a plan to bring night-and-day prayer to the forefront of the body of Christ across the globe in this hour?

Just as God has already set watchmen on the walls of Jerusalem, so too He has already established the fact that Jerusalem will become a praise in the earth. What does it mean? It is not simply that she will experience prosperity and peace, or that all of her inhabitants will be saved, although those things will take place. When the Lord says that Jerusalem will become "a praise in the earth," He is referring to a far greater reality. The only way that Jerusalem will become praiseworthy is when One who is worthy of praise is dwelling in her midst. Thus, He is referring to the day when Jesus' throne will be established in Jerusalem, making her the praise of the whole earth.

The Scriptures are full of verses declaring Jerusalem as the chosen dwelling of the Lord forever.[3] When Jesus returns, He is coming to set up His global empire—to establish the kingdom of God on the earth. Then and only then will Jerusalem truly be "a praise in the earth." Jesus will rule the planet from Jerusalem, and the nations of the earth will come there every year to worship the Lord.[4] Isaiah 2:3 prophecies that people will stream to Jerusalem to hear Jesus teach the ways of the Lord. How awesome it will be when our King, Jesus, proclaims God's word from Zion! Zechariah 2:5 foretells that Jesus will be the glory in the midst of Jerusalem. Oh, for the day that we see this with our own eyes!

We are living in an incredibly exciting time. The fact that God is establishing night-and-day prayer across the globe lets us know that the time of His return is near. I pray that these truths would sink down deep into your heart. Perhaps you are one called as a watchman in this most dramatic time. I pray you would clearly discern the Lord's direction for your life with regard to this noble calling.

Notes

1. 1 Chronicles 9:22.
2. Romans 8:14.
3. Psalm 48:1–8; 50:1–3; 132:13; Isaiah 60; Zechariah 1:14–17; 2:5, 10–12; 8:1–8.
4. Zechariah 14:16.

12

Kingdom Come

AFTER OBSERVING THE PRAYER LIVES of John the Baptist's disciples, Jesus' own twelve asked for a lesson on prayer. "Teach us to pray, as John also taught his disciples." Jesus' response is now repeated in church services on a weekly basis worldwide.

"Our Father in heaven, hallowed be Your name.
Your kingdom come.
Your will be done
On earth as it is in heaven.
Give us day by day our daily bread.
And forgive us our sins,
For we also forgive everyone who is indebted to us.
And do not lead us into temptation,
But deliver us from the evil one." (Luke 11:2–4)

The Lord's Prayer gives us an important format for prayer. However, because of our familiarity with it, we often mutter the words without considering their importance. At the crux of this prayer lies a familiar but incredibly fearsome concept.

In Jesus' primary teaching on prayer, He instructs His disciples to petition the Father for His kingdom to come and His will to be done on the earth in the same way it is done in heaven. In heaven there is no breach in God's sovereign reign and authority. There is not a moment of indecision among the heavenly hosts. Everything operates fully and completely by the ever-guiding direction of the

Creator. When we request that this type of rule be instituted in the earth, we must be prepared for God to intrude upon our own lives, at the very least, and to thoroughly devastate us, at the most. When we pray "Your kingdom come; Your will be done," we must understand that we are surrendering our kingdom and our will in favor of God's kingdom and will.

With this in mind, I think we need to compare Jesus' key lesson on prayer with our own view of prayer's purpose. Popular preaching often portrays prayer as a means to an end that ultimately serves our own needs. However, Jesus depicts prayer as a necessity to see *God's will* fully established on earth.

Rather than parroting liturgical jargon when we pray, we need to understand God's kingdom and what it means to pray in accordance with His divine intentions. God's agenda for prayer is far greater than our own purposes. He fully intends to answer the prayers of His people and establish His kingdom in every facet of every society. According to the prayer lesson that Jesus gave the disciples, His intention for prayer must also be our principal focus in prayer. Let us, then, examine more closely the comprehensive establishment of the kingdom of God in the earth.

The History of the Kingdom

From the time of creation, God ordained that His kingdom would one day cover the earth. When the "kingdom comes," the culture of heaven will permeate every earthly society with righteousness and justice. Additionally, out of God's great desire to partner with man, God has always intended man to rule His kingdom on the earth and to have dominion throughout the globe. To understand and embrace God's final plan for the establishment of His kingdom on earth, it is helpful to trace its development from Adam until now.

Adam

God gave Adam full dominion over the earth and its inhabitants. In doing so, He established Adam as the first man in charge of His kingdom on earth. However, when Adam sinned by disobeying God, he forfeited his earthly authority and dominion, handing it over to Satan.

Abraham

Approximately two thousand years after Adam's fall, God set apart Abram as part of the process of restoring man's place in His kingdom. His plan was to bring forth a nation, later called Israel, from Abram. God changed Abram's name to Abraham and told him that the number of his descendants would be greater than the stars in the sky. God's intricate plan included one day uniting the kingdom of Israel's descendants with the kingdom of God. In other words, a future king of Israel would be the chosen ruler of God's kingdom on the earth.

David

About one thousand years passed from the time that God called Abraham until the time that Israel's second king, David, reigned. After David became king, God prophesied that David would be part of an incredible family dynasty. In fact, God promised that *all* the rightful kings of Israel would come from David's line. Furthermore, God's own Son, Messiah, would come from the seed of David and would one day reign forever.

> "Furthermore I tell you that the LORD will build you a house. And it shall be, when your days are fulfilled, when you must go to be with your fathers, that I will set up your seed after you, who will be of your sons; and I will establish his kingdom. He shall build Me a house, and I will establish his throne forever. I will be his Father, and he shall be My son; and I will not take My mercy away from him, as I took it from him who was before you. And I will establish him in My house and in My kingdom forever; and his throne shall be established forever." (1 Chronicles 17:10–14)

David was the first king to rule the empire over which the Son of God would one day reign forever. It's a shock to our minds, but God promised David that God's own Son would rule and reign not only over the nation of Israel, but over God's kingdom on earth. As king of Israel, David knew that he was sitting on the earthly throne of the kingdom of God. David actually referred to his own throne as "the throne of the kingdom of the Lord!" (1 Chronicles 28:5; 29:23).

Daniel

After David's death, his son Solomon ruled Israel. But it wasn't long before Solomon disobeyed God by worshiping idols. As a result, the kingdom of Israel was eventually split in two, and the people began to turn away from God. Within four hundred years, they were completely decimated—carried away to Babylon in exile. Because Israel was no more, it looked as if there was no hope for God's chosen king to ever sit upon Israel's eternal throne.

But during the Babylonian captivity, God raised up Daniel as a prophet to explain His plan regarding Israel's future and the reign of the future king.

> "I was watching in the night visions, and behold, One like the Son of Man, coming with the clouds of heaven! He came to the Ancient of Days, and they brought Him near before Him. Then to Him was given dominion and glory and a kingdom, that all peoples, nations, and languages should serve Him. His dominion is an everlasting dominion, which shall not pass away, and His kingdom the one which shall not be destroyed." (Daniel 7:13–14)

Daniel's vision gave hope to Israel that although the nation was in captivity, Messiah was still coming. Daniel's visions became a source of great encouragement for Israel, giving them renewed hope in the earthly establishment of God's kingdom.

John the Baptist

John, the cousin of Jesus, was the forerunner of the coming king. His message could be summed up with one thought: "Repent, because the kingdom of God is here, now!" John declared to Israel that the kingdom of God was coming upon the earth, telling the ordained inheritors that they must change their lifestyles and the way they understood the kingdom if they were to receive it. John proclaimed that merely being of the chosen bloodline would not gain them entrance into the kingdom of God, for *all* men through sin had given their allegiance to the kingdom of darkness. John boldly warned Israel that her sins disqualified her from citizenship in the Lord's kingdom. She must now heed God's requirement of repentance to enter and participate in the kingdom of God.

Jesus

At the beginning of His public ministry, Jesus also proclaimed the coming kingdom and told people to repent of their sins. He manifested the kingdom's power through signs and wonders, confirming the authenticity of His claims that He was the Son of God and rightful heir of the kingdom. The Pharisees thought they could thwart Jesus' claims by having Him crucified, but Christ's crucifixion was the very act that forever sealed His rulership. Through His death and resurrection, He opened God's kingdom to all who would renounce the kingdom of darkness and embrace the values of the kingdom of God.

Jesus won back the authority that Adam had lost. This is why Paul referred to Jesus as the last Adam. Jesus has received from the Father all authority to institute His kingdom upon the earth, and He has called His church to disciple the nations in the values and principles of the kingdom of God. Our role is to establish the kingdom throughout the earth until the day Jesus comes to finalize its completion.

The kingdom of God is not an abstract reality. Jesus is returning to fulfill the promise made to David and to see His Father's will physically enacted upon the earth as it is in heaven. When Jesus returns, He will rule all nations as God's chosen king. He will take dominion and institute the values of the kingdom of God throughout the earth. Every facet of every society in every nation will be ruled by Jesus and embrace His value system.

Revelation 20 is the most well-known passage on the subject, but Scripture is full of verses referring to the reality of the returning King.[1] Daniel prophesied of a man "coming with the clouds of heaven . . . to Him was given dominion and glory and a kingdom, that all peoples, nations, and languages should serve Him" (Daniel 7:13–14). Jesus is the One who will return in power and glory to rule over this everlasting kingdom, on earth as it is in heaven.

The Necessity of Repentance

One does not have to wait until Christ's return before entering the kingdom of God. The way into God's kingdom is open now, and He has extended an invitation for all to enter. However, entrance is conditional upon repentance. To repent is to change one's mind, leading to changed actions. It is not good enough to simply "feel sorry"; sorrow must lead to a change in behavior. To truly repent, one must turn away from darkness and turn to God's light. When a person renounces his citizenship in the kingdom of darkness, confesses his sins, and chooses to submit himself fully to the values of the kingdom of God, only then does he truly enter.

Messages are often preached that offer forgiveness without calling people to repentance. When people run to receive mercy from God without repentance, they receive nothing, for there is no entrance to the kingdom of God without true repentance. They must voluntarily turn from darkness to be able to accept the offer of forgiveness through Christ's blood and thus enter the kingdom. Much damage is done when people are offered forgiveness of sin without the requirement of repentance. They willingly accept the offer, believing themselves to be saved, yet they continue living in sin. If a person never leaves the kingdom of darkness, how can he enter the kingdom of light?

The message of repentance is central to the gospel of the kingdom. Jesus identified the proclamation of this message as an important catalyst for His return.[2] Once the gospel of the kingdom is preached to all nations, Jesus will come and take possession of the earth.

God's Agenda

"I have set My King on My holy hill of Zion." (Psalm 2:6)

God has made up His mind that Jesus is His chosen King. Though the nations rage against God's choice,[3] His is the only vote that matters. Jesus is coming to initiate a global takeover of all the kingdoms of the earth. Though the kingdom of darkness currently prevails over the nations, a new kingdom has been inaugurated and is coming in fullness. In His mercy, right now, Jesus is extending an invitation to *every* nation to repent before He completes the establishment of His kingdom on the earth.

Jesus' worldwide empire will be far greater than any human empire that has ever existed. He will institute the value system of His kingdom throughout every nation. All nations will participate harmoniously in God's government, choosing righteousness over wickedness. And Jesus, as King of kings, will fully restore humanity's loyalty to God through His one-thousand-year reign of righteousness and justice.

After this one-thousand-year reign (known as the Millennium), the earth will be restored—realigned with God's holy ways. Paul says it this way, "He must reign till He has put all enemies under His feet . . . when all things are made subject to Him, then the Son Himself will also be subject to Him who put all things under Him, that God may be all in all" (1 Corinthians 15:25, 28). God will make His tabernacle with men, and the bliss of Eden will again be realized—this time on a global scale.

These plans are non-negotiable. The Father's intentions are already determined. He will not be influenced or intimidated. No man's opinion will cause Him to relent. He has already chosen Jesus to be the human leader of the kingdom of God on the earth.

This is a key issue in the Father's end-time agenda, and it is the very reason that Jesus instructed us to pray for the earthly establishment of God's kingdom when He taught us the Lord's Prayer. In essence, the church has been petitioning heaven to institute Jesus' earthly reign for over two thousand years!

What's more staggering is that the global prayer movement God is raising up today is focused on Jesus' return and the coming of God's kingdom. Never before in the history of the earth has God raised up a corporate, night-and-day cry for Jesus to return. This global symphony of prayer is beginning to move in harmony with the Father's will. With one voice, and in unity with the Holy Spirit, the bride is crying out, "Come, Lord Jesus!" (Revelation 22:17, 20).

It is amazing to consider that millions around the world are petitioning Jesus to return, fulfill the Father's plan, and take authority of the planet. He is going to answer this corporate cry in a definitive way. This is God's agenda, and right now the prayer movement is "hastening the coming of the day of God" (2 Peter 3:12), contending until the kingdom of God is fully established upon the earth. Oh Lord, let Your kingdom come, Your will be done, on earth as it is in heaven!

Notes

1. For example, Isaiah 2; 4; 11–12; 35; Jeremiah 33; Ezekiel 40–43; Zephaniah 3; Zechariah 2.
2. Matthew 24:14.
3. Psalm 2:1–3.

13

The Great Drama of the Ages

Now that we understand that Jesus is returning in answer to His people's prayers and that He will establish God's kingdom throughout the earth, it begs the question, how will this incredible drama unfold? The answer is both exciting and troubling.

Great blessing and great conflict are on the horizon. The forces of darkness and the forces of light are going to collide in a manner never before seen. Global revival, massive judgments, and incredible persecution will all happen in the last days. In this chapter, we will discuss the manner in which these events will unfold and the role the saints have in this final stage of human history.

The years before Jesus returns will feature a dramatic clash between demonically inspired kings of the earth and the kingdom of God. God will demonstrate the superiority of His strength and wisdom through the saints. His divine judgments will be released because of the intercessory cries of His people. Thus, the full consummation of history will come as a result of the unified prayers of His bride.

Satan will rage against believers and make war on the saints. God will release judgment events that will pound the kingdom of darkness. In that hour, the church will find herself vulnerable. Defenseless, naturally speaking, she will be compelled to pray. God will make use of the less-than-favorable earthly circumstances to cause His people to call upon His name. The only option for the church in that day will be prayer. God will remove all of the props she relies on for comfort in order to see the bride refined as by fire. Ultimately, she will emerge pure, spotless, and leaning on her Beloved.[1]

Prayer: The Catalyst and Response

This day of testing will come in response to the requests of a praying church for her King to return. And, in perfect irony, the Lord has seen to it that the only way to make it through this time will be through prayer. Fervent prayer will be both the catalyst and the essential response to the climax of this age.

Revelation 8 clearly portrays how the saints' prayers will work to initiate end-time events. An angel with a golden censer mixes all the prayers of the saints together with holy fire and hurls the mixture to the earth. The saints' prayers, mingled with fire, release God's holy judgments. A third of the earth's trees are then burned, along with all the grass. A third of the fresh waters and the sea become poisoned; the sun, moon, and stars are affected. Famine and war grip the planet as death freely runs its course, and men faint from fear. This dark day will be the precursor to the birthing of the kingdom of God on earth in fullness, and the entire scenario is *brought about by the saints crying out in agreement with God's will*!

Taking part in the administration of God's divine judgment affords the church an intimacy not granted to the rest of humanity. Jesus desires to rule and reign with His bride.[2] How amazing that He actually shares His government with His beloved! Our companionship with Him gives us authority in the heavenly courts of God's kingdom.

Not only do the saints *initiate* the Day of the Lord through prayer; they actually *hasten* its arrival. As we commit today to praying in agreement with Jesus, we quicken the day of His coming. Indeed, every prayer in agreement with His will fills the bowls of Revelation 8 and speeds the day of His return.

It is important that the church learns to be fervent in prayer before the Day of the Lord comes, for prayer will be our only viable response in that hour of crisis. Communion with the Judge, the

Man Christ Jesus, will be the church's sole mode of survival through tribulation. As the drama of human history comes to a crescendo, the bride of Christ *must* answer the crisis by abandoning herself to the only realistic option: prayer.

In that hour, the church will draw confidence from her foresight of the impending judgments. Just as prayer releases divine justice on the earth, prayer will also aid the end-time church in evading the effects of the judgments. Throughout Scripture, God turns His ear to those who cry out to Him in trials. David, Daniel, Peter, Paul, Silas, and John are all men whom God helped when they petitioned Him in times of great need. Although they still suffered, God shortened their trials, minimizing the effects because of their response of prayer and fasting. In the same way, He has promised to aid His church at the end of the age.[3]

When God's judgment comes upon the earth, rulers will flee and try to hide, but this will not bring them deliverance. The Antichrist will attempt to retaliate against God with his own battle plan, besieging Jerusalem with his armies.[4] However, his plans will be completely ineffective, regardless of the zeal with which he carries them out. A life immersed in passionate, fervent prayer will be the only means by which protection, direction, and provision can be obtained in that hour.

The Victorious Church at the End of the Age

"The accuser of our brethren, who accused them before our God day and night, has been cast down. And they overcame him by the blood of the Lamb and by the word of their testimony, and they did not love their lives to the death." (Revelation 12:10–11)

Understanding that the church will be triumphant at the end of the age is crucial to any study of the end times. Without this lens, the believer's approach to the end times will be the opposite of God's intention. God's consistent desire is to give men dominion on the earth, the way He did with Adam. Prayer is the prescribed method for such dominion to be established in the kingdom of God, both now and in the final years of this age.

Contrary to common belief, the church *will be victorious* through the events of the Great Tribulation. Though economically pressed and physically persecuted, the bride of Christ will overcome hardship by God's sustaining grace and power. She will live in communion with the One who initiates and administrates the tribulation, Jesus Christ. Thus, she will be granted deliverance through the time of trouble, similar to the way Daniel emerged from the danger of the lions' den. Because God has ordained this great conflict, the church need not fear. Rather, through prayer, she must draw confidence from her identity as beloved of the Lord, as well as from the fact that God has promised His people victory.[5] Though she lay down her life, even perhaps unto martyrdom, she will overcome Satan's attempts to cause her to lose faith. Jesus promised us that though we may die, we would not be lost.[6] We must adopt His vantage point of victory through trials.

Psalm 149 prophesies concerning a company of people who will partner with God in releasing judgment on the nations through prayer, describing such as a great honor.

> Let the high praises of God be in their mouth . . . to execute vengeance on the nations . . . to execute on them the written judgment—this honor have all His saints. (Psalm 149:6–7, 9)

At the end of the age, the church will fulfill this prophecy. Though the nations will rage against God and His people, the church will win this epic war through intercession. Worldly wisdom might consider prayer as a last resort to obtaining victory. But the saints will astonish the earth's inhabitants as God executes vengeance against the nations who oppose God on behalf of the church—all through the vehicle of prayer.

Just and True

"Great and marvelous are Your works, Lord God Almighty!
Just and true are Your ways, O King of the saints! Who shall
not fear You, O Lord, and glorify Your name? For You alone
are holy. For all nations shall come and worship before You, for
Your judgments have been manifested." (Revelation 15:3–4)

Revelation 15 includes a beautiful portrayal of the saints'
agreement with God's leadership at the end of the age. After all
the judgments are unleashed upon the earth, the church will still
confess that God is just and true! The church will call His works
and His ways, which include His judgments, great and marvelous.
Such a testimony, however, will be ludicrous to the nations, who
will be under the fierce judgments of the Lord.

Though martyrdom will sweep the earth and physical persecution against the saints will be unprecedented, God will empower
His people with grace to persevere. With the help and illumina-
tion of the Holy Spirit, God's people will anchor themselves in
His faithfulness, proclaiming His justice even amidst the most
horrifying circumstances.

The gospel will be proclaimed to the ends of the earth in that
hour. The result will be a harvest of souls the likes of which the
world has never seen. Revelation 5:9 depicts a great multitude before the throne of God, "out of every tribe and tongue and people
and nation." This means that a final harvest will touch every single
people group on the earth. At the time of this writing, some seven
thousand people groups have yet to hear the gospel.[7] However,
before the culmination of this age, the power of the gospel will
sweep through every people group on the planet, claiming for the
Lord the greatest harvest in history. Signs, wonders, and miracles
will accompany the proclamation of the gospel throughout the
nations, and masses will come into the kingdom.

The hymns of praise in the book of Revelation exhibit the future victory of the church through trials and tribulations. Over and over again, God's people praise and exalt His name, even though they have gone through incredible tribulation. The church will be a righteous remnant, agreeing with every facet of God's divine government in the generation of the Lord's return, and seeing kingdom power released in an unprecedented way.

Birthing the Kingdom

Just as birth pangs begin subtly for a woman who is near childbirth, so will the judgment events begin that will culminate in this age. Almost indiscernibly at first, birth pangs begin to prepare a woman's body to deliver her child. The mother wonders, "Could this be it? Am I in labor?" So too will judgment events begin to prepare the earth for the end of this age. In childbirth, the pains intensify, becoming great contractions that leave no mistake that the child is on its way. Likewise, the subtle pains of creation will turn into full-scale labor, which will result in Christ's return and the birthing of God's kingdom in fullness.

The earth is already experiencing the initial phase of birth pangs. In His perfect wisdom, God will use these trials to cause His bride throughout the nations to seek Him in night-and-day prayer. It will be the epitome of counterculture for the church to respond positively and prayerfully to the calamities taking place on the earth. The church will be the sole entity proclaiming His goodness in the midst of end-time judgments and intense persecution.

Many unbelievers will be convicted and converted, while many others will respond by accusing and cursing God. He will be portrayed as wicked in His administration—One who causes calamity and curses humanity. Yet God's perfect leadership and mercy will bring the greatest number of people to salvation through the least severe means possible—He will give all the earth a chance to repent before it is too late. He will gather in a great harvest of new saints, remove all areas of compromise from His bride, and judge the impenitent. The end-time landscape of trial and challenge will be the ideal context for Him to perfectly execute His will and enthrone His Son.

Playing Our Role

Whether voluntarily or involuntarily, Jesus will ultimately have the compliance of every individual upon the earth. Scripture declares that *every* knee will bow and *every* tongue will confess that Jesus is Lord.[8] Every eye will see Him when He returns,[9] and the Father will give Him the nations as His inheritance.[10] God has given people the liberty to choose partnership with His Son, even now. And prior to Jesus' earthly establishment as king, believers are offered the unique gift of entering into dynamic partnership with His purposes through prayer.

It is our highest privilege and honor to partner with our King by praying His will. Furthermore, we are assured of future partnership with Christ. Jesus said that those who overcome will sit with Him upon His throne ruling the nations in the next age.[11]

In regard to His coming, Jesus warned His disciples not to be caught unaware, but rather to watch and pray for their master's return.[12] Clearly He is encouraging us to engage with His plans and with His heart, to stay alert and be ready through prayer and fasting.

In the parable of the ten virgins, the guests heard the cry, "The bridegroom is coming!" (Matthew 25:6). Those who had prepared were ready to meet Him, but those who had not were found wanting, and in the end were unable to enter the wedding feast. Those who desire to participate with Jesus at the end of the age must *prepare now* for their role in the coming great drama. Prayer is the great preparer as well as the sustainer of the redeemed at the end of the age.

The call is going forth—the bridegroom is coming! But are we ready for Him? The earth will face an unprecedented time of power, grace, trial, and calamity. When we look at the current state of the church, can we say with confidence that we are prepared for the coming days of judgment and harvest? I pray that many would find themselves watching and ready to meet the challenges and blessings of the coming days.

Notes

1. See Song of Solomon 8:5; Ephesians 5:27; 1 Peter 1:19.
2. Revelation 1:5–6; 20:4.
3. Matthew 24:22.
4. See Revelation 6:12–16; cf. Joel 3:2, 12; Zephaniah 3:8; Zechariah 12:2–3; 14:2; Revelation 16:14.
5. See Jesus' exhortations to the seven churches in Revelation 2–3, "to him who overcomes."
6. Luke 21:16–18.
7. joshuaproject.net.
8. Philippians 2:10–11.
9. Revelation 1:7.
10. Psalms 2:8.
11. Revelation 3:21.
12. Mark 13:33, 35–37.

14

The Anna Anointing

Now there was one, Anna, a prophetess, the daughter of
Phanuel, of the tribe of Asher. She was of a great age, and
had lived with a husband seven years from her virginity;
and this woman was a widow of about eighty-four years,
who did not depart from the temple, but served God with
fastings and prayers night and day. And coming in that
instant she gave thanks to the Lord, and spoke of Him
to all those who looked for redemption in Jerusalem.

LUKE 2:36–38

A Day Like No Other

TAKE A MOMENT AND LET your mind wander—what was it
like the day that Anna came face to face with God in the
flesh? Imagine the sense of awe that Anna must have felt the moment she realized that she was looking at the fulfillment of over
sixty years of fasting and prayer as she peered into the face of
the Messiah. To gain a clearer picture of Anna's journey we must
consider where it began.

We are introduced to the prophetess on the day that she first
beheld the baby Jesus. It was no accident that this woman met
the Messiah. In other words, Anna didn't just happen to be in the
temple that day—her lifestyle was one of continual prayer and
fasting, interceding for Israel's Messiah to come. This moment was

the culmination of sixty years of intercession, a lifetime of prayers all answered in an instant.

Anna was married as a young woman. According to the International Standard Bible Encyclopedia, "tradition says that the tribe of Asher was noted for the beauty and talent of its women, who for these gifts, were qualified for royal and high-priestly marriage."[1] It is likely that Anna was a very beautiful and gifted young lady. It is also likely that she had married a notable young man, who was probably well esteemed and equally gifted. For seven years she enjoyed the blessings of married life with her husband. At the height of joy, the unthinkable happened. Tragedy struck and she found herself in one of the most difficult situations life can offer: her beloved husband had died suddenly. The Bible gives us no information as to his cause of death. All we know is that while Anna was still young and had a life full of promise ahead of her, she was left a widow. How would this young woman emotionally and mentally cope with this catastrophe? What was left in life that could offer her anything close to the bliss she had experienced in her young life with her husband?

In the moment of her greatest crisis, Anna made an amazing and wise decision. Rather than pursuing other options, she determined to devote herself to fasting and prayer. She wholeheartedly pursued God to such an extent that it was said of her that she "never left the temple." In what was probably the most pivotal and challenging time of her life, she made the wisest decision one can make. She gave herself to a lifestyle of prayer and fasting, clinging to God and God alone.

It is remarkable that Anna's decision was not simply a momentary impulse; instead, it was a choice that shaped the rest of her days. Having decided to seek the Lord, she found herself in the place of prayer for a year, and then two. Two years turned into five, and five turned into ten, ten to twenty, and then many more. This radical, persistent life of abandonment to God in prayer and fasting led to the day when Anna found herself peering into the face of the Son of God.

Anna's heritage actually foretold her journey. She was the daughter of Phanuel, whose name literally means "face of God."[2] Anna's name literally means "grace."[3] Allegorically speaking, Anna's life was destined by the grace of God to see the face of God.

We know that God does nothing in the earth unless He reveals it to His servants the prophets.[4] Since Anna was a prophetess, it is likely that she knew by prophetic insight that her constant intercession would culminate in the revelation of Messiah on earth. I believe that she had "seen" the day many times in her spirit, yet now she was experiencing it with her natural eyes. Perhaps as she came into the temple that wonderful day, everything seemed strangely familiar. Her mind raced as she pondered, "Could this be the day?" She rounded the corner and saw what she had seen in her heart many times before, but this time it was actually happening right in front of her—Simeon was prophesying over the baby, the God-man, Jesus. And in a moment, the entire purpose of her life was fulfilled.

From that day forward Anna told all who were looking for redemption in Jerusalem about Messiah. Some scholars believe that she went door to door throughout all Israel proclaiming to any who would listen that Messiah had come in the flesh.

A Prophetic Picture

This remarkable woman's life is a prophetic picture for the church today. Just as God released grace upon Anna to fast and pray until she saw the first physical revelation of Jesus to the earth, God is releasing a similar grace upon a whole generation of believers who will operate in a similar anointing, interceding for the next revelation of Jesus to the earth—His second coming. God is igniting a prayer movement all over the earth, which will usher in the greatest revival, along with the greatest tribulation, that the planet has ever seen, leading up to the return of His Son. The anointing that rested upon Anna will rest upon multitudes of believers before Jesus' second coming

Anna operated in a unique threefold anointing. First, she was clearly an intercessor; she "served God with fastings and prayers, night and day" (Luke 2:37). It is important to note that the Lord identified Anna's lifestyle of fasting and prayer as *valid* service to Him. Fasting and prayer were part of her regular life of intimacy and devotion to the Lord. Anna had given herself to hearing God's heart and praying His desires back to Him, which in fact is what prayer is at its core—hearing God's heartbeat and praying His desires back to him.

Next, Anna operated as a prophetess. Being a prophetess does not only mean that one has an anointing in revelatory gifts. Most of the prophets in the Old Testament operated in *all* the realms of the Spirit of God, with signs, wonders, and miracles. We can assume that Anna had both a revelatory and a power ministry.

Thirdly, Anna was also clearly an evangelist. Once she had seen the Lord Jesus, she "spoke of Him to all those who looked for redemption in Jerusalem" (Luke 2:38). She had drawn close to the Lord in partnership with His heart through fasting and prayer, and had moved in the power of the Holy Spirit. Once she saw Jesus, she began to proclaim the truth about the Messiah to any who would listen.

In the earth today, God is equipping an entire generation with a similar threefold grace and anointing. This generation transcends age and gender; it includes both male and female, young and old. These are people who will give themselves to fasting and prayer as a lifestyle. As Anna did, they will make the wisest choice in the hour of the earth's greatest trial. They will give themselves to fasting and prayer to see God's face revealed in power when Jesus returns to the earth.

Like Anna, the people of this generation will operate in the power of the Spirit of God. They are the prophetic generation of which Joel prophesied—an entire company upon whom God will pour out His Spirit.[5] They will manifest the power of the kingdom, moving in signs, wonders, and miracles, and will see the great harvest of souls at the end of this age.

Finally, this generation will be broken for the lost. They will be filled with zeal to proclaim the gospel to all who will listen. With thunder in their mouths, these messengers will declare, with authority, the reality of the risen Christ. The Spirit of the Lord will be upon them as on no other generation in history. They will fast and pray, preach and prophesy, which will result in God releasing His power in the earth, gathering untold millions into His kingdom.

Calling Forth the Annas

A young man once said to me, "I think I've got it. It's not fasting *or* prayer; it's fasting *and* prayer." I agreed. Anna clearly understood this, and has become a heroine to all who desire to operate in a similar anointing. Her example inspires courage in those who yearn to live lifestyles of fasting and prayer, and to powerfully proclaim the gospel. God is stirring the hearts of many right now to make radical life decisions like Anna did. He is calling for prayer and fasting to be the main priority in their lives.

We are living in an hour in which the Lord is calling forth the "Annas." I believe that just as Anna's intercession resulted in the first coming of the Lord Jesus, this end-time assembly of Annas will precipitate His promised return.

If you feel a stirring in your heart toward this lifestyle, it is likely that the Lord is calling you to make the same type of decision that Anna made. While the earth is in turmoil, God's prophetic alarm is sounding, calling believers to fast and pray, by His grace, as their main pursuit. From the soil of persistent prayer and fasting, God will release the greatest thrust of power and evangelism the earth has ever seen.

Is the Lord stirring your heart, like he did Anna's, to spend your days seeking Him in worship and prayer with fasting as your primary focus? The final thrust of the gospel into the hardest and darkest places of the earth will be carried out by radically abandoned lovers of God, ones like Anna, who have given themselves to pursuing God in long, loving hours of worship and prayer.

I believe we have a short window of time to respond to the Spirit's call to watch and pray. The final act in the epic drama of this age has already begun. If the Lord is moving on your heart, I encourage you to make the necessary changes so that you may heed the Spirit's call.

Notes

1. *International Standard Bible Encyclopedia,* s.v. "Anna'" by James Orr, ed., Bible History Online, accessed December 4, 2014, http://www. bible-history. com/isbe/A/ANNA.

2. Roswell D. Hitchcock, *Hitchcock's Bible Names Dictionary,* s.v. "Phanuel," Bible Hub, accessed December 4, 2014, biblehub.com/dictionary/p/phanuel. htm#hit.

3. International Standard Bible Encyclopedia, s.v. "Anna."

4. Amos 3:7.

5. Joel 2:28–32.

15

The Joel 2 Mandate

"Turn to Me with all your heart, with fasting, with weeping, and with mourning." So rend your heart, and not your garments; return to the LORD your God, for He is gracious and merciful, slow to anger, and of great kindness; and He relents from doing harm.

JOEL 2:12–13

T HE BOOK OF JOEL IS invaluable at this time, in light of the upheaval in the nations and the escalation of sin in society. The world is in turmoil, while humanity's rebellion against God intensifies. Joel gives us a biblical template of the prescribed lifestyle for people who live in times of great turmoil and face the judgment of God. Joel portrays powerful truths, dealing not only with Israel's history, but also with the future Day of the Lord.

The Prophetic Plague

In chapter 1, the prophet describes a plague of locusts that have completely destroyed the land, leaving Israel reeling from its devastating effects. Our Western minds cannot comprehend the destructive power of a locust plague.

Imagine a swarm of locusts appearing with a haunting hum and the buzzing of beating wings. The swarm darkens the sky like an eclipse as the hordes of insects blot out the sun's rays. As they devour the crops, they sound like a raging fire devouring a forest. Even more frightening than their appearance is the devastation they leave in their wake. A swarm of locusts can number in the millions and cover hundreds of square miles of land. A single swarm is capable of consuming thousands of tons of food in one day, wreaking havoc on entire regions.

However, it was not merely *one* swarm of locusts that was released upon Israel in Joel's day; there were *four* successive swarms, which pummeled the land, one after another, until Israel was completely ravaged. The crops were destroyed, leaving the nation with no grain or oil, no stores of food. These common staples were a source of food and energy for the population, and were used for offerings in the temple.

As food and energy supplies were cut off, Israel's society suffered the consequences. Offerings had to cease in the temple. Livestock began to starve to death in the open fields. To make matters worse, a drought came upon the land. The scorching heat of the sun caused brush fires, which consumed the stubble that had been left by the locusts.

The only possible remedy for this massive ecological crisis was for the land to be drenched in showers of refreshing rain. God promised He would pour out rain upon Israel's dry land if His people would turn to Him with all their hearts.

In chapter 2, Joel tells the people to sound an alarm and gather the multitudes together for a solemn assembly of fasting and prayer. This is the only posture that could bring relief for God's people. Joel urges the Israelites to repent and turn back to the Lord with all their hearts so that God would heal their land.

The Ultimate Judgment

Joel then stuns his hearers with a shocking word from the Lord. The chilling message was this: though the locust plague was extremely severe, it was not the final judgment. He tells them that the locust plague was only a prophetic picture of the *real* judgment that would come upon them if they did not return to the Lord. He said that an exceedingly fierce and destructive army was coming—the Babylonians.

The Babylonian army was well known for the devastation that they brought upon the surrounding nations. As they conquered neighboring lands, they tortured and murdered the people and burned their cities to the ground. They were the most feared and savage military force of that day.

Joel told the Israelites that just as the locusts had destroyed the land, the Babylonians would devour Israel and incinerate everything in their path. He told them that though they had undergone an initial measure of judgment, a greater judgment was coming. The only way to avert it was for God's people to assemble in fasting, prayer, and repentance—to return to the ways of the Lord.

In response, the people entered into a season of repentance and revival after the preaching of Joel, and God brought healing to the land (during the reign of King Josiah). However, their repentance was spiritually shallow and short-lived. They soon returned to their idol worship and rebellion. Because they refused to heed the warnings of Joel and other prophets, they ended up coming under the exact judgment the Lord had decreed. The Babylonian army swept down upon Jerusalem in three different waves, conquering it in less than twenty years.

The sad fact is that Israel need not have experienced this judgment. If the people had turned to the Lord with their whole hearts, the Lord would have relented. When God sends messengers to warn His people and the people do not heed those warnings, God's only choice is to release judgment. He does this because of the covenant He has with His people. He will not allow them to continue in their sin, but will do whatever is necessary to get their attention, so that they turn their hearts back toward Him.

The Plagues of Our Generation

The book of Joel should be an unsettling warning to us in this generation. Many people focus on the promise of the outpouring of the Spirit when they read Joel.[1] But they are almost completely unaware that this promised end-time outpouring is going to come as a stroke of mercy just *before* the great and terrible Day of the Lord, God's final judgment upon the earth. The Day of the Lord will shake the whole earth to bring vindication to the righteous and retribution to the wicked.[2]

Joel's prophecies have not yet been completely fulfilled. The fearsome words of chapters 2 and 3 proclaim that a season of global judgment against all the nations is coming. God used the Babylonian army as an instrument of judgment against Israel. This is a prophetic picture of a future army that is coming at the end of the age—an army that will be led by Antichrist himself. God will use him as an instrument of judgment, just as He used the Babylonians (and other invaders throughout Israel's history). Antichrist will devour the nations and demand that the people worship him as God. This coming day will be the greatest day of tribulation the earth has ever seen.

In our generation, we have watched sin escalate to a level the world has never seen. We live in the first generation in which the wholesale murder of infants is acceptable and protected by law in many parts of the world. We live at a time when millions of people are held as slaves,[3] exploited sexually and for labor—more than at any other time in the history of the world. Homosexuality has been embraced as an alternative lifestyle. Pornography is available on demand through the Internet. Biblical signs of the end of the age are being fulfilled before our very eyes.

In the United States, we claim to be a nation "under God," yet it is obvious that we have greatly strayed from the foundational truths of Christianity. We must be honest about the state of the nation if we are ever going to see change. My goal is not to blame or shame, but rather to provoke and compel us out of complacency.

It has become commonplace in the church to seek large crowds and the praise of men while ignoring the core values of the kingdom of God, such as meekness, mercy, and hunger for righteousness. We are concerned with becoming "relevant" to a wicked world, rather than being the light of the world and the salt of the earth. If we are, as Jesus put it, salt without its flavor, how can we be effective in transforming the lives of the lost?[4] We must stop associating church growth with revival. We must not confuse the success of mass marketing appeals with the authentic move of the Holy Spirit, which convicts and converts the hearts of men.

Because of the state of our nation and, more importantly, the state of the *church* in our nation, I believe America stands in danger of significant judgment. We have effectively signed up for God's judgment by slaughtering babies, embracing homosexuality, and becoming the world's largest purveyor of perversion and pornography. Yet it appears that we are asleep. Let us not forget that as of this writing we are only thirteen years removed from the catastrophe of 9/11, and just nine years from the tragic events of Hurricane Katrina, which rendered the entire Gulf Coast of the United States powerless. Within the last year, terrorist armies of the Islamic State (ISIS) have declared war on Israel and the United States and put to death thousands of Christians in the Middle East. The first wave of locusts has begun to descend upon us, and we are oblivious to the fact that destruction has come and is still coming.

Many are living in a state of spiritual delusion, intoxicated by religiosity, yet with waning evidence of an authentic faith. We compromise our Christian walk by being intertwined with the world, yet we believe that we are safe and secure in our salvation. How we need a true, God-birthed revival that turns the hearts of the masses to the Lord!

How Should We Respond?

Our only hope is to embrace the lifestyle outlined in Joel 2. I believe a trumpet is sounding in the Spirit right now, calling us to return to the Lord through fasting and prayer, weeping and mourning. We must repent fully and turn to the Lord with all our hearts. Then we will see the spiritual darkness that has possessed our nation overthrown, and revival released. Joel 2 is clear: solemn assemblies devoted to fasting, prayer, and repentance are the only antidote for the judgments that are sure to come upon our nation—indeed, any nation.

As we have discussed, God is raising up companies of believers throughout the earth who are coming together in ceaseless intercession. The most productive and biblically sound way to address the issues that we face in our day is through fasting, prayer, and repentance. When communities gather under the banner of Joel 2 and engage in night-and-day prayer, they are, in essence, living in a perpetual solemn assembly. If we embrace Joel 2 as an end-time mandate, God will hear our cries, have mercy on our sin, and release a great move of His Spirit.

Some may ask, "How practical is it to live a *lifestyle* of fasting and prayer?" For some, being part of a perpetual solemn assembly might mean connecting with a community of believers who take turns as watchmen on the wall. Some may have jobs that occupy much of their day, but will still do their part, praying alongside fellow believers two, five, ten, or more hours per week. Others will give themselves full-time to intercession, making prayer and worship their vocation. Throughout the earth, many people are being commissioned by the Lord to serve Him in fasting and prayer as their full-time occupation, like the Levites of old.

The issue is not *how* you engage with the Lord in prayer, but simply that you do. It is of critical importance that we find ourselves fasting and praying, seeking the Lord while He may be found. This is the hour. We must make living in a culture of prayer our way of life, and petition the God of mercy.

Who Can Stand?

The probing question asked in the book of Joel is this: "For the day of the Lord is great and very terrible; who can endure it?" (Joel 2:11). A great shaking is coming to the earth.[5] Who will be able to stand? A Joel 2 lifestyle is the key to being able to endure in that day. When we give ourselves to fasting and prayer, and in tenderness turn our hearts to the Lord, God will hear our cries and release mercy to us. He not only *loves* mercy; His very *name* is mercy.[6]

Whether you pray two hours a week, or fifty, becoming part of a community of believers who seek the Lord continually through prayer and fasting is essential. Scripture is clear that many will fall away during the coming time of great crisis.[7] Ultimately, those who are able to stand firm at the end of the age will be those who love truth and are given to prayer. The spotless bride for whom Jesus will return will be a praying bride.[8]

Can You Hear the Sound?

The question for us now is, will the church heed the call to fast and pray? Will we hear the alarm that is sounding in the Spirit, calling us to embrace the Joel 2 mandate? Can we hear the sound of the locust wings beginning to hum? Will we perceive the darkness that has begun to cover us? The catastrophes that we have seen in the last decade are only the beginning of what is coming. But as we give ourselves to prayer and fasting, God will answer with mercy and release the promised outpouring of His Spirit, which will literally usher millions into His kingdom.

Night-and-day prayer affords us the opportunity to not only hold solemn assemblies, but to live our lives continually in worship and prayer—to intercede for the kingdom to come and the bride to be ready. While many may have strategies for church growth or "relevant outreaches," these strategies alone are not going to stem the tide of the judgment that is coming upon our nation. The Joel 2 mandate is vital to the global prayer movement, uniting all believers in a cry for mercy. The alarm is sounding, and we must heed the call.

Notes

1. Joel 2:28–32.
2. 2 Thessalonians 1:6–10.

3. Estimates from varying sources range from 12–30 million.
4. Matthew 5:13.
5. Haggai 2:21–22.
6. Exodus 34:6.
7. 2 Thessalonians 2:3; 1 Timothy 4:1.
8. Revelation 22:17.

16

How Now Shall We Live?

THE EVIDENCE IS COMPELLING. NIGHT-AND-DAY prayer is not only a biblical pattern for worship; nor is it simply a historic practice occurring over generations in the church; but it is sweeping the globe in our generation. Never has there been a movement of prayer that even remotely mirrors the current movement. What's more, in addition to giving us faith for great spiritual breakthrough in our day, the biblical precedents and promises attached to night-and-day prayer declare the fact that the greatest day the planet has ever seen is directly before us—the second coming of the Lord.

I remember the first time these truths began to become clear to me; what had been previously hidden from my eyes was now as plain as day in the Bible, and my heart was compelled to seek the Lord in a new way. The more I studied, the more truths I discovered that demanded a response. I wanted to pursue Him with all my heart.

When I first heard of night-and-day prayer, I thought it was an incredible waste of time. I never envisioned myself participating in it and definitely did not see myself leading a community rooted in night-and-day prayer. Honestly, I could not understand why someone would want to pray all day. It's funny how the Lord has a way of directing us into the very thing we would rather avoid.

Now, nearly fifteen years later, my desire to seek Him is still growing. I am more convinced than ever of God's leadership in my life and of His masterful orchestration of plans to culminate this age in partnership with a praying bride.

Within the last few weeks, as I've been finishing up the edits to this book, I have heard of houses of prayer in some of the most closed nations on the earth. God is penetrating darkness everywhere with night-and-day prayer. Like pinpricks of light streaming through a darkened sky, houses of prayer and praying churches are dotting the map in every nation. What an incredible time to be alive.

Though the tide of darkness is rising, there is cause for great hope in this hour. The tidal wave of prayer God is raising up will soon crash upon the earth as revival across the nations. The greatest move of God's Spirit is still to come. Untold millions will come to the knowledge of Jesus as Savior and Lord.

Throughout the pages of this book I have illustrated the biblical and historical precedents for night-and-day prayer while also sharing biblical arguments for night-and-day prayer as a lifestyle. From the life of David, to God's plan for Israel's redemption, to Anna as a prophetic picture, to Joel's call for solemn assemblies, to Jesus' own words, "My house shall be called a house of prayer"—the Scriptures are bursting with encouragement that perpetual prayer is a valid and prescribed practice for the people of God.

The question before each one of us is, what will I do? Now that you are armed with the necessary information and the biblical foundations, how will you respond?

The first and easiest response is to take a critical look at your schedule and see where you can redeem time that is being wasted. Schedule time in prayer daily. Make it your most important appointment of the day. Be extravagant. Ask God for grace to stretch you and diligence to walk it out.

Next, connect with a praying church or house of prayer. It doesn't necessarily have to have a twenty-four-hour worship and prayer meeting, but look for a place that embraces the value of prayer. Ask the Lord to direct you to a community that prioritizes God's presence above other ministry endeavors. Only that which is born of prayer is of value in the kingdom. Connect with a spiritual family that shares this pursuit.

Finally, feed your heart on messages that will encourage you in the place of prayer. I have found that intimacy with God, revival, the end times, and the Sermon on the Mount are all topics that give my heart an urgency to pray.

Jesus is worthy of our love. He is worthy of a life laid down. I don't believe we have time to continue to do church as usual. Instead we must heed the call to "seek the Lord while He may be found, call upon Him while He is near" (Isaiah 55:6). This is the hour! I encourage you to seek Him night and day until He rains righteousness upon the earth.

---┤ **APPENDIX** ┝---

Was Worship 24/7 in the Tabernacle of David?

W E KNOW THAT THE DAVIDIC pattern of worship took place day and night. Some accept this as twenty-four-hour-a-day worship before the ark of the covenant. Others challenge this position, believing it took place regularly but not ceaselessly. I believe the scriptural indications, as well as the volume of scholarship, point to the tabernacle of David operating in unceasing worship and prayer for the duration of David's reign. My reasoning is as follows.

1 Chronicles 16:37 states that Asaph and his relatives were stationed before the ark the day David brought it into Jerusalem to minister to the Lord in worship "*continually*, as every day's work required" (NASB).

The word translated "continually" is the Hebrew word *tamid*. Brown-Driver-Briggs Hebrew Definitions gives the following meanings for *tamid*: continuity, to stretch, continually, perpetuity, continuously.[1] Strong's Greek and Hebrew Definitions informs us that the word is from "an unused root meaning to stretch" as in the sense of indefinite extension.[2]

1 Chronicles 9:33 says the worship took place "day and night" before the ark.

Regarding "day and night," Albert Barnes says the singers were "free . . . from any special duties besides those of supervision, which was so arranged among the overseers that someone exercised it during every part of both day and night."[3]

From John Wesley's Notes on 1 Chronicles 9:33: "Day and night - Continually, and particularly in the morning and evening, the two times appointed for solemn service. Thus was God continually praised, as it is fit he should be, who is continually doing us good."[4]

From Matthew Henry's Commentary on 1 Chronicles 9: "Thus was the temple a figure of the heavenly one, where they rest not day nor night from praising God, Revelation 4:8. Blessed be His name, believers there shall, not in turn, but all together, without interruption, praise him night and day: may the Lord make each of us fit for the inheritance of the saints in light."[5]

In commenting on Isaiah 62:6, "I have set watchmen on your walls, O Jerusalem; they shall never hold their peace day or night. You who make mention of the LORD, do not keep silent," Adam Clarke refers to 1 Chronicles 9:33 saying, "The image in this place is taken from the temple service; in which there was appointed a constant watch, day and night, by the Levites: and among them this seems to have belonged particularly to the singers, see I Chronicles 9:33."[6]

In addition, the template for David's tabernacle was the tabernacle of Moses, requiring that "the fire on the altar shall be kept burning on it; it shall not be put out" (Leviticus 6:12). It seems evident that David employed God's desire for a continuous sacrifice to burn through utilizing singers and musicians to provide the sacrifice—in other words, the fruit of their lips giving thanks to His name in night-and-day, continual worship and prayer.

In my view, there is sufficient scholarship and textual evidence to support the idea that night-and-day ministry to the Lord in the tabernacle of David was, in fact, twenty-four hours a day, seven days a week. Therefore, I have used the terms "night-and-day worship and prayer," "24/7 worship and prayer," and "unceasing worship and prayer" synonymously.

Notes

1. Francis Brown et al., *The Enhanced Brown-Driver-Briggs Hebrew and English Lexicon: with an Appendix Containing the Biblical Aramaic* (Oak Harbor, WA: Logos Research Systems, 2000), s.v. "tamid".

2. James Strong, *Strong's Exhaustive Concordance of the Bible*, updated ed. (Peabody, MA: Hendrickson Publishers, 2007), s.v. "tamid".

3. Albert Barnes, *Notes on the Old Testament* (Grand Rapids: Baker Books, 1998), s.v. "day and night".

4. John Wesley and G. Roger Schoenhals, *Wesley's Notes on the Bible* (Grand Rapids: Francis Asbury Press, 1987), s.v. "1 Chronicles 9:33".

5. Matthew Henry, *Matthew Henry's Commentary on the Whole Bible* (New York: F. H. Revell, 1935), s.v. "1 Chronicles 9".

6. Adam Clarke, *Commentary on the Holy Bible* (Nashville: Abingdon, 1977), s.v. "Isaiah 62:6".

DID YOU ENJOY *UNCEASING*?

Recommend the eBook to a friend. Available for Kindle, Nook, and iBooks

ihopkc.org/unceasing

ANOTHER RECOMMENDED BOOK FROM BILLY HUMPHREY
To Know Him

Who is God? It's a question people have asked since the beginning of creation. And even after thirteen years in ministry, Billy Humphrey was confronted one day with the fact that he didn't really know God—not intimately, not deeply, not in the way his heart craved.

In *To Know Him*, Billy describes his incredible journey into the knowledge of God that transformed every area of his life.

God has designed each part of our lives to teach us spiritual truths about Himself. This book offers a fresh revelation of God's heart by addressing the question "Who is God?" in marriage, in parenting, in finance, in work, and in ministry. Once you know and see God in each area of your life, it will completely and radically change the way you see the world.

Billy Humphrey is a man of tremendous integrity, authority, and pioneering perseverance that has led to insightful revelation of God and His kingdom. This book is both inspiring and practical and is sure to leave the reader with the motivation to hotly pursue God and to joyfully line one's life up with the truth.

—Andy Byrd, Director, Fire and Frangrance, YWAM, University of the Nations, Kona, Hawaii

For speaking engagements and additional resources, visit **billyhumphrey.com**

INTERNATIONAL HOUSE *of* PRAYER

· ·

24/7 LIVE WORSHIP AND PRAYER

ihopkc.org/prayerroom

· ·

Since September 19, 1999, we have continued in night-and-day prayer with worship as the foundation of our ministry to win the lost, heal the sick, and make disciples, as we labor alongside the larger Body of Christ to see the Great Commission fulfilled, and to function as forerunners who prepare the way for the return of Jesus.

By the grace of God, we are committed to combining 24/7 prayers for justice with 24/7 works of justice until the Lord returns. We believe we are better equipped to reach out to others when our lives are rooted in prayer that focuses on intimacy with God and intercession for breakthrough of the fullness of God's power and purpose for this generation.

The Best *of the* Prayer Room Live

SIX LIVE WORSHIP ALBUMS PER YEAR

· ·

Every other month we release a new volume of worship
and prayer recordings from our Global Prayer Room.

Subscribe today at **ihopkc.org/bestof**

International House of Prayer Missions Base, 3535 E. Red Bridge Road, Kansas City, MO 64137
(816) 763-0200 | info@ihopkc.org

INTERNATIONAL
HOUSE *of* PRAYER
UNIVERSITY

MINISTRY · MUSIC · MEDIA · MISSIONS

ENCOUNTER GOD. DO HIS WORKS. CHANGE THE WORLD.

ihopkc.org/ihopu

International House of Prayer University (IHOPU) is a full-time Bible school which exists to equip this generation in the Word and in the power of the Holy Spirit for the bold proclamation of the Lord Jesus and His return.

As part of the International House of Prayer, our Bible school is built around the centrality of the Word and 24/7 prayer with worship, equipping students in the Word and the power of the Spirit for the bold proclamation of the Lord Jesus and His kingdom. Training at IHOPU forms not only minds but also lifestyle and character, to sustain students for a life of obedience, humility, and anointed service in the kingdom. Our curriculum combines in-depth biblical training with discipleship, practical service, outreach, and works of compassion.

IHOPU is for students who long to encounter Jesus. With schools of ministry, music, media, and missions, our one- to four-year certificate and diploma programs prepare students to engage in the Great Commission and obey Jesus' commandments to love God and people.

> "What Bible School has 'prayer' on its curriculum? The most important thing a man can study is the prayer part of the Book. But where is this taught?
>
> Let us strip off the last bandage and declare that many of our presidents and teachers do not pray, shed no tears, know no travail. Can they teach what they do not know?"
>
> –Leonard Ravenhill, *Why Revival Tarries*

International House of Prayer University, 12901 S. US Highway 71, Grandview, MO 64030
(816) 763-0243 | info@ihopu.org

International House *of* Prayer
INTERNSHIPS

INTRO TO IHOPKC • FIRE IN THE NIGHT
ONE THING INTERNSHIP • SIMEON COMPANY

ihopkc.org/internships

Internships exist to see people equipped with the Word of God, ministering in the power of the Holy Spirit, engaged in intercession, and committed to outreach and service.

Our four internships are three to six months long and accommodate all seasons of life. The purpose of the internships is to further prepare individuals of all ages as intercessors, worshipers, messengers, singers, and musicians for the work of the kingdom. While each internship has a distinctive age limit, length, and schedule, they all share the same central training components: corporate prayer and worship meetings, classroom instruction, practical ministry experience, outreach, and relationship-building.

Biblical teaching in all of the internships focuses on intimacy with Jesus, ministry in the power of the Holy Spirit, the forerunner ministry, evangelizing the lost, justice, and outreach. Interns also receive practical, hands-on training in the prophetic and healing ministries.

Upon successful completion of a six-month internship or two three-month tracks, some will stay and apply to join IHOPKC staff.

Our IHOPKC Leadership Team

Our leadership team of over a hundred and fifty men and women, with diversity of experience, background, and training, represents twenty countries and thirty denominations and oversees eighty-five departments on our missions base. With a breadth of experience in pastoral ministry, missions work, education, and the marketplace, this team's training in various disciplines includes over forty master's degrees and ten doctorates.

International House of Prayer Missions Base, 3535 E. Red Bridge Road, Kansas City, MO 64137
(816) 763-0200 | internships@ihopkc.org